AF413279

THE SHADOWS WITHIN MY LIGHT

A JOURNEY OF DISCOVERY AND FAITH

A MEMOIR

MICHAEL EDWARD ANTHONY

*It is my firm belief that angels exist and that they walk among us.
Their assignments may vary in scope and duration, departing
this earthly realm when called away at its completion. To my
adopted parents, without whom I would never have come to
know the light.*

PROLOGUE

"I promise to tell the truth, the whole truth, and nothing but the truth, so help me God!"

"Growing drowsiness caused my eyes to slowly close, my thoughts scattering into the dark shadows and the pain loosening its hold. Overwhelmed by the never-ending torment, I yearned to enter the door of sleep without end."– M.A.M.

Throughout my six decades on this Earth, I have faced numerous challenges due to my ethnicity, lineage, preferences, and decisions. Despite these obstacles, I have accomplished many things, achieved various goals, and encountered countless compelling individuals along the way. However, I must admit that I have far too often put myself in detrimental situations.

Life was drama free and prosperous during times of tranquility. Eventually, by fate or flawed judgments, distressing situations would occur. Depending on their depth, instant solutions were only sometimes possible.

Getting out of some dilemmas became a matter of survival. Not creating new troubles became the ultimate test.

When I think back through all those years, times of struggle outnumber times of success. Memories of the more pleasant moments sometimes arise. However, the ominous difficulties can also emerge in moments of reflection and occasionally in my dreams. A picture, a place, or a song can also induce troubling memories; thoughts of regret occur when I question what could have been.

Almost all my wants and wishes have been realized; little else remains. I have even done things others would not do for the thrill or by involuntary persuasion. It is humbling to have lived through all the odds encountered, many against my well-being. There is, however, one last goal to achieve: I must honor a promise made.

1

ALL BUT FORGOTTEN

Before The Enlightenment

My earliest memory dates back to 1962, when my parents took me to a party when I was about four years old. It didn't take long for us to get there because the location was only a few streets away. Music filled the night sky, guiding us like a beacon to the celebration. People had parked their cars on the road and in the yard; it was apparent that the crowd was sizable.

It was a typical Upper Midwestern spring night, with a gentle, warm breeze blowing as we walked from the car up to the modest-size home. Somebody knocked loudly on the door, and when the door opened, we entered a smoke-filled room where people were standing and sitting, laughing and talking.

The music came from the other room, so I walked to the wall, looked around, and saw more people dancing, laughing, and having a ball. Almost everybody at the party had cans in their hands, which, as it looked, made them feel happier. There's not much more I remember about that night, and even though I try, I can remember only a little of what came before.

Not long after that, I attended another celebration organized by relatives we often visited in the big city. Our cousins lived upstairs in the two-family house, so almost everyone was there when we arrived, and others came in time. I know it was a birthday party because I remember the balloons and the cake; I believe it was for my mother's sister. They sectioned off a small area in the basement for the chairs, where I was sitting, and the table for the cake and essentials. They used what was left of the modest basement as the dance floor.

I couldn't help nodding to the beat of the music because it was the same as the music played at the other party. Several people saw me and persuaded me to dance, so I got up and walked onto the dance floor. That night was the first time I ever danced, and I loved it; it felt natural. Mom and Dad had returned upstairs, so they didn't get the chance to see me. Everyone clapped and cheered when I finished, so they must have enjoyed my dancing as well.

Another faint memory comes to mind as I reflect on those days. My mother's niece, who cared for me when I was a toddler, and I were walking along one of the main streets in our neighborhood one day. As we strolled along, we came across an enormous concrete double staircase. When we reached the stairs, I separated from her and ran up one side of the stairs and right back down the other. Later, someone told me that the building was a church. At that age, I did not know about churches. As a result, I was not intrigued by the establishment itself but rather by the steps leading up to it.

Not long after that, we moved to the home I remember. It was a large two-story house on a corner lot next to a dead-end street. The front door entered the sitting room, where we watched television, and the stairs to the left led to the bedrooms upstairs. To the right was the living room, to the left was the dining room, and my parents' bedroom off the dining room. The last room was the kitchen, which had doors to the back porch and basement.

I especially liked the basement because it had a trap door to the backyard. The backyard was the width of the house, extending several yards to the property line; the rest of the yard, on the left side, was enormous. Manicured bushes wrapped around the front and one side of the yard, and large shrubbery and small trees lined the back of the property. I remember my father cutting the grass and bushes a few times, and when I grew tall enough, he taught me how to do it.

At first, we had an old lawnmower with blades that spun when we pushed it. Cutting all that grass with that lawnmower took a lot of energy, effort, and time. Dad eventually bought a gas-powered mower, which made cutting all that grass easier and less time-consuming. He finally upgraded to a riding lawnmower, which made cutting all that grass almost effortless and more fun. Plus, it was like driving a little car, which I loved; it prepared me for the real thing.

As for all those bushes, which comprised around 3/4 of the property, we first used handheld manual hedge clippers to maintain them, which required a lot of upper body and arm strength. Then, Dad invested in electric hedge clippers, and an exceptionally long extension cord, significantly easing the entire process and enhancing precision. The only concern was avoiding accidentally cutting that long extension cord during the process. I fancied myself a sculptor because when the job was complete, it resembled the work of a professional. It was my responsibility to maintain that huge yard, and I made sure it looked immaculate.

~

LIKE MOST CHILDREN MY AGE, I liked playing with toys, fiddling with stuff, taking things apart—like old radios— and riding my bicycle and motorbike all around the neighborhood. I also enjoyed watching television, and I watched it a lot. Aside from cartoons, I mostly liked science fiction, suspense, mysteries, horror, and comedy shows. I was also involved in sports, like when I played pee wee football. Our team practiced at the corporate ballfield downtown. Even though we were pee wees, it gave me a sense of being a professional football player because it was a regulation-size stadium.

I was a modest-sized child, and I was quick on my feet, so they put me in the position of offensive running back. It was the perfect position for me, but, unfortunately, I quit after playing for a brief time. During practice one day, three people tackled me simultaneously from three different directions. It was apparent I wasn't fast enough. One hit me on my shoulders, one at my waist, and one at my feet. It felt like they broke my body. I cried out in agony, and the coaches ran onto the field to see if I was okay. As I lay there, severe pain surged all over my body, but nothing was broken or sprained.

My pride was hurt because of my status as a prominent player on the team. My father's pride was damaged as well. When he had the chance, he said, "You cried like a baby. I was embarrassed and ashamed of you." He also shared other sentiments to express his displeasure with me. The coach switched me to a defensive position, and I didn't do too badly, but I wouldn't say I liked it as much as running the ball. I asked, but the coach wouldn't put me back on offense again, probably because of that three-point tackle. So, considering all that, I decided to end my pee wee contact football career.

I OFTEN USED my speed in friendly rivalry against my friends in the neighborhood. When we played in the area, we ran everywhere. We held races in the street and ran from one location to another to play. I usually crossed the finish line or got to our destination first, but there were times when I almost didn't make it. My best friend, Rob, who was slightly overweight, always tried to slow me down. When it was time to run to another location, he would yell, "Let's go!" while swinging his fist with all his might into my stomach.

His backhanded gut punch hurt, but his strategy rarely worked. After desperately gasping for air to catch my breath, I ran as fast as possible to the destination. There was only one time I didn't make it there first. That's when I finally grew tired of him gut-punching me, so I got smart and started anticipating his enthusiasm and sidestepping his attack. He stopped trying to hit me in the stomach after that.

The woods surrounding the city landfill close to our neighborhood were a destination we often ran to. We explored every inch of the woods, running and tripping over tree roots, stepping in mud, climbing trees, and getting stuck and scratched by branches. We looked under rocks and boulders and moved dead trees to see what was living beneath them. There was always something to look for and discover in the dark, intricate, and mysterious woods —a curiosity-seeker's dream.

My impulsiveness, need for adventure, bold nature, and avid curiosity sometimes tested my parents' patience. To be truthful, I often tested my parents' patience. My father called me hard-headed because I usually did what they told me not to do. Whatever consequences I faced didn't matter; I needed to do what they told me not to do because they sparked my interest by telling me not to do it.

They warned me often to avoid certain situations and not put myself in harm's way. When I didn't heed those warnings, the harsh discipline happened. Occasionally, my dad sat me down to talk before the action began. I hated those talks the most. I didn't want to discuss why I was getting punished; I already knew. It was a one-sided discussion anyway. He asked me questions like "Didn't I tell you not to leave the yard?" Or "Didn't you hear me when I called you?"

I tried to answer truthfully because he somehow knew when I lied. The lie spankings were always relentlessly intense.

Sometimes, he took me into the bedroom and shut the door behind us, then he blocked the door so I couldn't run back out. When he started swinging, I ran around the room as fast as possible, trying to hide behind furniture to escape the lashes. I couldn't hide in the closet because the door would be closed, so I would drop to the floor and crawl under the bed, hoping he couldn't reach me. He would yell, "Get out here!" after unsuccessfully trying to get at me. At that point, I had no choice. It was a command. So, with significant reluctance, I would come out and let him finish.

My mother used to discipline me as well. Her way was to hit me upside the head using the hand with the ring on it.

Since my hair was cut so short that I was almost bald, when her hand with the ring hit, it echoed in my brain and made me dizzy. I usually fell against something or stumbled a few steps away because of the force of the slap and dizziness. One time, I fake stumbled across the room and fell on the couch as if in a daze after she slapped me. She couldn't help but laugh at my acting skills, and, to my delight, she decided not to finish disciplining me for whatever I had done.

One day, one of my parents overheard my friend and me discussing a punishment my friend had received. It was clear they had heard us because they decided a similar discipline was in order when I eventually got in trouble again. My friend and I both had a toy called Hot Wheels. It came with two small cars, along with orange plastic strips that connected to make the racetrack.

My parents thought using one of the plastic strips like my friend's parents did would be a suitable change from the switches and belts they whipped me with. The marks are still visible, especially on my upper arm. They never hit me with the plastic racetrack again after seeing the blood pouring from the cut it made on my arm, and I stopped playing with my Hot Wheels toy after that dreadful experience.

ONE TIME, not long before my fifth birthday, I had pushed my mom too far, and the usual slap on the head wasn't enough. While I continued to argue with her, she said something strange to me. She told me that if I didn't start acting right, she would take me back to the children's home and let them deal with me.

I was confused. *What is the children's home?* I wondered.

Later, after she calmed down, I asked her to tell me what she had meant.

She explained to me how I became their child—that they had adopted me because she couldn't have children. She went on to say that I had been misbehaving so badly that she was considering returning me. *Would my mother really take me back to a children's home for being bad?* I wondered. I didn't know what to feel about that. I know that her threat made an impression because I can still see in my mind the exact spot in the house where she said it.

How am I supposed to feel about my birth mother abandoning me? Why did she give me up? I wondered. *Who is my biological father, and where is he?* I also wondered. Fearing that Mom might send me back to a children's I couldn't recall and troubled by the knowledge that my birth parents didn't want me, I was burdened with these thoughts deeply for some time.

There is, however, one line I did not cross. I did not disrespect my parents in any way, especially not after they forcefully showed me the error of my choice to do it once. My impulse to talk back to them was also cut short under similar circumstances. In retrospect, I must admit that those harsh and plentiful punishments did shape the type of person I would become. I can't imagine how I might have been without my adoptive parents' loving discipline.

My parents were strict. Perhaps this was for a good reason, but I was happy and thankful to be with them. They loved, supported, and provided for me as if I were their own. If they hadn't told me I was adopted, I would never have known. As a young child, finding out I came from someone else posed more questions, like *Whom do I take after, my father or mother? And which one do I look like?* At the time, none of my questions would be answered; only in the future would the answers be revealed. As for now, my life was comfortable and secure with my parents.

After what seemed like years of avoidable punishments, it became clear that the time had come to change my ways, especially after finding out about my adoption at five years old. I have always admitted that I received many punishments; I knew how I was and often deserved them. So, I designed a solution. If I wanted to avoid more trouble and punishment, I would either obey my parents or better hide the truth about my activities. For the latter, I learned to lie more convincingly and did not lie as much, leading to a significant decline in punishments.

MY STATUS as an only child changed when I became a brother at the age of five. I welcomed my sister lovingly; she had long, soft, curly hair, the cutest giggle, and a precious, dimpled smile, and she was always happy. Now that I had a sister, I knew I would always have someone to play with when she got older. I enjoyed pondering how we might play outside and eventually run around with friends. Until then, while she was still an infant, she drew my parents' attention away from me and my activities.

After she started getting around well, running all over the house, and getting into everything, Mom would tell us to go outside to play. Once, we sneaked away from the neighborhood to see our cousins on my dad's side. We got caught when my sister told on us, but she didn't know she wasn't supposed to expose our whereabouts. After that, we asked for permission, and my sister usually kept quiet about some of our activities. However, she was sometimes eager to tell our parents I had done something wrong. One day, she didn't have to tell because we obviously returned home after the streetlights came on.

Our parents scolded us and grounded us for days, which was unbearable, given my desire to play outside. Though my punishments had decreased, I now had a partner. When we got in trouble together, the scolding was more for me than her, and I knew that. She was my little sister, and I was her big brother. It was my responsibility to watch out for her no matter what. But we still managed to have fun when outside. However, that grounding encouraged me to start getting her home on time.

One day, when we finished one of our adventures, I nicknamed her "Wild Woman" because of how her hair looked. Her curls twisted in all directions, with twigs and leaves sticking out everywhere. She was a sight to see. She hung in there with me no matter what we did and played as hard as I did wherever we went. She was my sister, friend, and partner. We were quite the pair.

A FEW YEARS LATER, in 1968, when I was nine years old, my little brother arrived on the scene. He was a chubby bundle of life, with plump cheeks and an irresistible giggle, his head covered in a multitude of loose jet-black curls. I still vividly remember the day my father cut his hair. As the first curls fell to the floor, I felt devastated despite it not being my hair. Most of the hurt was for my little brother; his hair was beautiful, and he would never get to know it. My dad kept cutting it, as he did mine, in a semi-bald bowl cut. His curls never grew back.

Being the youngest, he had to play catch-up, and as he grew, he caught on just fine. He got away with all types of things. When he did something wrong, he didn't get disciplined like I did. To my frustration, when I told my parents about something he had done, they often didn't react the way I hoped they would.

Once, he was acting out after my parents left the house, so I locked him in their bedroom until they returned home. I'm sure you can imagine what happened to me. Eventually, I accepted defeat and realized he was the baby in the family and could, and usually would, get away with anything. Nevertheless, despite our complexities while growing up, we established sibling adoration for each other over time.

My mom worked in nursing for as long as I can remember. I think it was the only job she ever had. Whenever we hurt ourselves, she was there to fix us. I remember the time I used my bed as a trampoline. I jumped, and jumped, and jumped, and suddenly, one leg missed the bed, and I fell face-first into the backboard, busting my bottom lip wide open.

I ran through the house crying, dripping blood everywhere, and screaming for my mother. When I found her, she calmed me down and tended to my injury without delay. It still hurt and was still swollen, but at least it stopped bleeding. Come to think of it, I often kept Mom busy tending to my many childhood injuries. The scars and bruises below my knees tell some of that story; that's why I don't wear shorts.

Daddy worked as an electrician at an aerospace facility; he installed the electrical wiring in the blimp cabins. I was always curious about the big black oval hangar my dad worked in, but as badly as I wanted to, I never got the chance to go inside to see a blimp close up. I was once able to see a little of the interior of the hangar through one door when we picked Dad up from work, but I didn't see a blimp inside. Whenever I see one floating in the sky, I think of my father. It makes me proud.

I remember when my dad used to play with me; he tickled me a lot. I was ticklish, and he liked hearing me laugh. He tickled me so hard and long sometimes that I would wet myself. I couldn't help it because he wouldn't stop even after I told him I was getting ready to do it. If Mom said I couldn't do something or go somewhere, I went to ask Dad if I could. He always said, "What did your mother say?" My disappointment was usually obvious, so he would say something funny and tickle me to take it away, which changed my disposition.

My dad's other talents were drawing, painting, and portraiture, which I picked up by observation and some of his instruction. He was also skilled in remodeling. He worked on our house and other buildings, and I played a significant part as his young apprentice. I learned much about remodeling from my father, but I didn't know how to tell him, or even if I should have, that the occupation did not appeal to me. I wouldn't say I liked doing it at all.

My DAD's company held this grand yearly Christmas party for all the employees. The building hall was huge, with massive rooms and extremely lofty ceilings. The Christmas tree was gigantic and reached up almost to the ceiling. The entire hall was ornamented with incredible decorations. Hundreds of toys lay around the tree and on tables around the room. Each child got to pick one present, and there was always a toy I wanted. Christmas goodies lay on other tables, available for every person there, and everyone mingled pleasantly, sharing in the season's cheer.

Our Christmas tree at home always had many presents under it as well. Somehow, our parents (I mean Santa) managed to bring everything we wanted every year. Trying to sleep on Christmas Eve was almost impossible. When Christmas Day arrived, we woke up to Christmas music playing, the smell of baking cookies, and the sounds of breakfast being prepared in the kitchen. We jumped out of bed, ran from our rooms, and headed straight to the tree. All presents were unwrapped in record time, and we began playing immediately.

As the day progressed, most family members arrived to take part in the holiday dinner at our home. Everybody seemed joyful, discussing past gatherings and catching up on current events. When the last family members arrived, dinner was served. Everyone made the rounds, stacking as much food as possible on the sturdy paper plates. Then they found their place to sit and eat. It makes me feel sentimental to reminisce about the family all sitting together at the dining room table and in various chairs around the room, eating, talking, and laughing.

In those days, when Christmas Day arrived, the ground was usually covered with thick snow. My cousins, friends, and I played outside all day until dinner. We had snowball fights, made snow angels and snowmen, traversed snow-covered yards, jumped in snowdrifts, and ran in the streets, running in the slush, getting it all over us, and then sliding to see how far we could go. Those pure moments are all but forgotten, but I will cherish what I remember of them forever.

OUR ADVENTURES SLOWED after the city demolished the garbage dump and the surrounding woods to build a city park and housing to replace the projects. The park was almost in our backyard, just one house away at the dead-end street beside our property. At the end of that street, they made a big hill three blocks long. In the winter, we had great fun riding on our sleds down the entire length to the end.

They also built tennis and basketball courts and installed playsets, like climbing bars and slides. The activities building is where they put the Carom and Ping-Pong tables. I first liked spinning around and getting dizzy on the merry-go-round they set up. A few kids got on, and another person turned it as fast as possible to see who would stay on or fly off. I flew off it once. Yes, I got hurt, and no, I did not ride it again, although I did become a spinner.

Getting in trouble didn't happen much anymore with the dump and woods gone. We played either in the park or our yards. One day, my sister and I were playing with two neighbors who lived across the street when one of them said something that made me laugh uncontrollably. I fell to the ground, doubled up in pain, and couldn't catch my breath. After a while, the spasms stopped, and my breathing returned to normal. That was the first time I had laughed that hard; it felt like I was dying.

On another occasion, I played with my new neighbors, who had recently relocated from the southern part of the country. Sometimes, as we played, it wasn't easy to comprehend what the one with the strongest Southern accent said. At one point, as we continued playing and conversing, he said something I didn't understand.

I asked him to repeat what he had said, and he did, but

even then, I struggled to grasp his meaning. His brother finally walked up to me and explained.

"Yonder," he said as he pointed. "Let's go yonder means let's go over there."

That was a surprising moment of insight for me. I found their accents and words intriguing, and their pleasant personalities made them enjoyable to be around.

One year, someone built a new house across from my friend's home at the end of the dead-end street. Eventually, we became acquainted with the new homeowners and their son. We welcomed them into our community and him into our neighborhood club. We all got along well, and he and I developed a bond of friendship that, over time, made his parents comfortable enough to invite me into their home. He had some cool toys to play with, and we often wrestled playfully when his parents weren't home. In our eyes, kids were kids, no matter their appearance or background. We were just kids.

While wrestling with my other best friend in a neighbor's yard one day, I ended up on my stomach, and he ended up sitting on my back. He grabbed me under my chin and pulled it back hard to get me to say uncle. He pulled so hard that I could hardly breathe or speak. Suddenly, I heard and felt my backbone pop. After fearfully moaning in panic, I yelled out, and he finally got off me. To my surprise, I wasn't paralyzed. Even when we played hard, sometimes hurting each other in the process, we settled our differences and continued to do as kids do. We had fun.

~

In 1969, when I was ten, my parents bought a swimming pool. Since our yard was huge, they put it in the back corner, and Dad built a deck around the top. I often got in the pool, jumping off the deck to make a big splash or just splashing around to cool down and have fun. It was also a chance for me to teach myself how to swim. Sometimes, my dad helped me, and I diligently watched the people swimming on television. I must have caught on because my parents signed me up to join the YMCA. With the added help of their instruction, I learned to swim exceptionally well over time.

Having a swimming pool in the yard was a novelty then; I knew we were fortunate. When my aunts, uncles, and cousins visited in the summer, we had big pool parties. Most everyone came ready with their swimwear and eventually got into the pool before the day ended. The children in the neighborhood used the pool the most. We played hard, splashing each other, dunking each other's head under, and wrestling to see who was the strongest in the water. We made sure to enjoy this luxury to the fullest.

A couple of us guys had talked about it and finally decided to go skinny-dipping in the pool one warm summer night. We couldn't be loud, splashing around and making much noise, because we were not supposed to be in the pool after dark. We quietly floated on the rafts, play-wrestled, or moved slowly around the pool, feeling the water against us. It was so peaceful, relaxing, and serene; there was also a revealing physical reaction.

Sometimes, while wrestling or playing with a friend one-on-one, I found myself in situations where the same reaction occurred. At first, I experienced confusion as to what had happened or why. It startled me. Sometime later, I was told that the experience was the physical response to bodily contact during adolescence as our bodies change due to puberty. In addition, my strong attraction to specific male friends made me feel self-conscious. What appealed to me as a young boy was the opposite of what was supposed to appeal to me, yet it all felt natural, and I didn't understand why.

Most of my friends were male, but I did have a few girl-friends at various times. One of them was rough-and-tumble; she liked to play hard. We even had the same last name, so she wouldn't have to change hers if we married. Ultimately, it didn't work out due to insufficient interest on my part. She was also slightly taller than me, so we were mismatched anyway.

My other girlfriend was beautiful. She was my dream girl—soft-spoken and petite with butterscotch-cream skin and beautiful, long, wavy jet-black hair. She was a concern for my father, who decided it was time to have "the talk" with me. The result of the conversation was for me to stop seeing her because I could get her pregnant.

After the talk, even though it was difficult for me to do so, I stopped visiting her. I was alarmed by the thought of having a baby at ten years old. If that part of me were to become excited, there was another way to deal with it: one-on-one with a friend. That was my reasoning and my solution to that problem. Grownups considered this alternative attraction irregular, yet it felt natural to me. *Will it go away when I get older?* I wondered. Maybe, maybe not. Even so, after considerable thought, I chose to keep the attraction subdued to avoid potential issues.

Light-Formed Foundation

My parents stopped attending parties and suddenly started attending church after my sister joined the family. I'm not sure why they decided to start going; as it turned out, my father's family were devout church worshipers with strong spiritual beliefs. My dad's father was a minister, and my grandmother was a prominent church member. We began attending regularly, and with my parents' change in consciousness came new rules and behaviors.

They started playing church music on the radio, replacing the other music they had once danced to. My mother caught me listening to what they now called "secular music."

"We don't listen to that type of music anymore," she said sternly, making it one of my parents' first declarations. They had played that music at the parties, and I loved it. I didn't want to stop listening. So, what I did was, at bedtime, I put the radio under my pillow with the volume low and listened until I fell asleep. The first song I learned by heart was "Come See About Me" by Diana Ross and The Supremes.

I thought I was getting away with it, but they probably saw that the radio wasn't on the table next to the bed when they came to my room to check on me. It became clear that they knew I was still listening to that music, and I'm glad that, for whatever reason, they didn't try to stop me from listening to it again. They eventually acknowledged my musical interest in a supportive way. It appears they came to notice that ability in me.

THE CHURCH WAS in a neighborhood close to where we lived. When we arrived, we parked in the lot across the street from the church. Others also arrived by car, and several nearby members walked; we joined them as they came. Watching all those people entering the church building made an impression on me. It was a special day for family and friends to come together in worship, and we were now a part of it.

Church gatherings were nothing like the party gatherings my parents had taken me to. Nobody brought their happy cans with them; all the men wore their best suits, and some women wore big hats and long dresses. Everyone seemed joyful, cordial, and on their best behavior. The congregation consisted of separate families, making every Sunday a big family reunion.

Sunday school for the children was where I headed. The entrance was through the church's back door. Aside from the typical childhood activities, like playing with plastic blocks, coloring, drawing, and painting, we listened to our teacher read Bible parables and discussed their meaning. The teacher also taught us about the magnificent miracles performed in biblical days, which totally captured my attention. I wondered why they got to see miracles in the Bible days and we didn't see them in our days. I wanted to see or experience a miracle in my lifetime. But would it be magnificent like those in the Bible?

As soon as Sunday school was over, all the kids made a mad dash through the basement to the back door. We ran up the stairs, slamming the door open when we reached it, jumped five steps down from the door, and hit the pavement running. It was recess time for us before the long church service started. We played a different game every Sunday; they were meant to tire us out so we would sit still during the service.

When recess ended, we ran to the church's front door. People would already be in the sanctuary for adult Sunday school, and others would walk in from the entrance hall. We squeezed and dodged through them to get to where our families were sitting. Every family sat together, and most had their favorite places. As the music played and the music director started greeting us, it was time for us to sit down. The choir marched in and stood at their benches, and then the ministry walked in and sat in their seats.

You can guess which part of the service I liked best. Many songs that the choir sang could be found in the hymnals, so we had all the words and music. They also had Bibles available in case someone forgot theirs at home. Service often began with the whole church joining in song. The music director started the service by saying, "Everyone, turn your hymnals to page 103," and the singing began. Music and voices filled the building with a glorious sound, and we usually sang more than one song.

Since the hymnals had words, the songs were easy to learn. I listened to the secular music every day and night, and I sang along with the church music during service; it all eventually paid off. The music director noticed my ability and asked me to sing with the children's choir. Our sound was that of little angels who visited Earth to sing just for that church. Over time, they asked me to sing a solo. I wasn't expecting that. All those people looking at me made me nervous; it was intense. Even so, being me, I was not easily deterred, so I stepped up confidently and sang that song passionately until the end. It became my mother's favorite song for me to sing—"Great Is Thy Faithfulness."

After the congregation finished singing, it was time to pray. An elder would walk up to the pulpit, greet everyone, and ask them to turn their Bibles to a specific verse. Then everyone read it together. They then would ask everyone to stand and bow their heads in prayer. Every person who started praying in church always began by saying, "Dear God," "Dear Heavenly Father," or "Dear Father in Heaven." The next phrase uttered was "We come to you today." From there, the prayer continued with thanks, requests for healing, and anything else the person felt they should say. Sometimes, it seemed like the prayers would go on forever.

What else seemed to go on forever was some of the preaching. Each minister's style was unique, and each picked a topic they believed they should share, often going over their allotted time. Some stood at the pulpit, spoke solemnly, and didn't venture far. Others might start moderately. But as they continued, their energy increased, and they eventually used the whole stage for effect. Certain preachers' voices periodically grew louder, reaching the volume of a yell. They might jump up and down or walk the aisles, exciting the congregation. Regardless of the delivery, when all the preachers finally finished sharing their messages, the Spirit made everybody in the church say, "Amen!"

When we visited other churches, they welcomed us to participate in their worship services. Most were sister churches with the same ethnicity as ours; others were the same except for being composed of another ethnicity. Even with this distinction, the theme of their services echoed ours. Their prayers were calm yet impassioned and sincere; some songs were sung similarly, and others were sung differently. Deliveries of the sermons differed moderately; the preachers often spoke with even tones and subtle energy. Even so, the message was delivered effectively, and the Spirit made everyone in the church say, "Amen!"

ONE CHURCH in a small nearby city offered my father a ministerial position after both of my parents became ministers. Everyone seemed happy for my father; it was a spiritual calling. I knew that leaving my church friends would be difficult; we would no longer see each other on Sundays and during the week, but I was curious about this new church and whom we might meet. It would also be a chance to experience a different city, so there was some eagerness about the transition.

Our new church's building resembled the old churches on television, with one room as the sanctuary and the basement below. Family members and neighbors made up the small congregation. They welcomed us enthusiastically. I can't describe the depth of kindness they showed when we arrived. My dad had no problem taking on his responsibilities; he even got to preach a few times. And during the church Women's Day observance, my mom was asked to speak. Dad was also called upon to use his remodeling skills for renovations needed in the church. Of course, I was his young apprentice, but this project would be a bit different.

WHEN WE ENTERED THE CHURCH, the atmosphere stood still and tranquil. It was God's house, with only the two of us in attendance. Our task was to renovate the church to restore its former newness. After turning on the lights, we set up the stands and gathered the equipment, then the measurements began. Dad told me where to hold the boards. Then he spread the measuring tape and marked off the dimensions. Next, he picked up the saw, placed it at the wood mark, and pressed the button. Whatever tranquility that did exist was utterly shattered by the buzz of that saw.

Sawdust quickly layered the workplace floor, shifting as we walked through it. The smell of freshly cut lumber filled the air as the hammering and the saw slicing the wood echoed beyond the building's walls. Every board and panel was carefully nailed into place at every cut and angle with precision. I don't remember how long it took. It must have taken a while since it was only my dad and me. Yet, in the end, no one would have known it was the work of only an adult and an eleven-year-old child..

I remember being in the sanctuary during the service and looking around at what my father and I had achieved. It filled me with pride, and I developed a new respect for remodeling. The Sunday after completing the project, they prepared a dinner to show their appreciation for our accomplishment. Whenever they had dinner at the church, the smell of the food downstairs joined us upstairs in the sanctuary. This distraction made it challenging to focus on the service or the decor as I thought about the food downstairs. Even though the view was inspiring, I couldn't wait for the service to end.

A small kitchen was in the back of the basement, with a serving counter to the right; the rest was open space. Most families in the small church brought something. The hosts put the food on the counter and a nearby table. A line formed when all the dishes were in place, as it was time to eat. I couldn't help noticing the mountain of food packed on everyone's plates. They usually ate all of it and then dessert. I must admit it couldn't be helped because the food tasted wonderful.

I always looked forward to Sunday dinners. They were the best.

THIS NEW LIFE did alter my relationships with my friends. I wasn't around my old church friends anymore, and, as for my other friends, I was told not to play with certain kids or go to certain people's houses. "They aren't Christians like we are," I was told. "Their ways are not like ours." Maybe because we started attending church, my parents thought something was supposed to change in me and I would become tarnished by being around certain kids. I felt no change, so it was difficult for me to understand their thinking.

As a result of this new sheltering, I was encouraged to choose my friends sensibly. I couldn't be around or bring home just anybody.

Speaking of "their ways," during sermons, the preacher often referred to people who didn't attend church as engaging in "worldly or wicked ways." He said they were sinners due to their worldly and wicked behavior. Hearing the phrase *worldly ways* often fed my curiosity. It brought back memories of dancing, laughing, and having a ball. As children, only occasionally did we observe adults drinking alcohol at family gatherings. But we didn't think much about it. They told stories, reminisced, laughed, joked, and danced, but they didn't overdo their consumption or get unpleasant at any time.

While gazing out the church window, I tried to imagine their ways. If going out and having fun, like at those two parties I slightly remembered, was wicked, I didn't understand why. I needed to experience their ways to comprehend why they were so bad. On the news, they told us about terrible things some people had done, but that was only a few individuals. They also showed people without homes and those who were fortunate, but I didn't know how others lived or what they did when they didn't attend church.

A part of me longed to experience the world's ways; I wanted to see everything. *How different would the people be?* I wondered. *What do they do when they are not attending church? What is it that they do that makes them sinners?*

My eagerness grew as I yearned to learn everything about worldly ways, yet that opportunity was years away. Until then, I contented myself with the joys of childhood: playing with friends, attending school, participating in family activities, and going to church every Sunday. Additionally, we frequently spent time with fellow church members and attended various gatherings throughout the week. We also went to a variety of services during the week.

Midweek prayer services or meetings were held every Wednesday night at both churches. Not as many people attended as on Sundays, so the mood was calm and earnest. Some church members held prayer meetings at home on certain days throughout the week. An even smaller number of people attended, and the atmosphere was humble and reverent. A few of us children came on different days; they kept us quiet by letting us play with toys or making us participate in a portion of the meetings. I was not too fond of the last part.

THIS DENOMINATION of churches also held a camp meeting every year at a retreat located in a nearby state. Hundreds of people from churches nationwide came to attend the massive vigil. It was a week-long event, with Christianity as the central theme. The tabernacle was the most prominent building on the campground, holding hundreds of fellow worshipers. Aside from the exciting first and last Sundays, they conducted small services and classes in the building several times daily, every day of the week.

Though long—some dull but others not—all sermons and classes delivered many teachings, instructions, and countless examples of how we should conduct our daily lives. They also warned of the probable consequences of disregarding sound judgment and basic upright behavior. The Bible Scriptures produced visions of splendor, suffering, healing, despair, wonders, conflicts, and triumphs. Every depiction in the Bible's New and Old Testaments has a meaning and a purpose. Comprehending the Scriptures' principles and applying them to our lives can bring healing, prosperity, contentment, and perseverance, which is what I came to believe it all meant.

Across the yard from the massive tabernacle were concession stands, where people went after the classes and services to get hot dogs, dinners, snow cones, ice cream, and other treats. I would see the feeling of inspiration, unity, and completeness on everyone's faces as they conversed. Scattered groups of people would begin walking to their cabins, mobile homes, or tents, fellowshipping as they dispersed.

When we finished eating our snow cones, we would run around the campground, playing and discovering until it was time for us to go in. Back at our trailer after dinner, full and tired from playing, we would lie on our beds, listening to the sounds of crickets hiding in the darkness of the tree-formed canopy. We were lulled to sleep by their mesmerizing sound, which was restful, peaceful, and deep.

For many years, my life consisted of the church establishment twenty-four hours a day, seven days a week. Everything was church, prayer meetings, the Bible, Bible studies, God, Jesus, Satan, the angels, the commandments, the disciples, the prophets, etc. My parents had turned away entirely from the secular life and fully embraced this Christianity. As for myself, I was a growing child and highly susceptible to any knowledge presented. Aside from my faint recollections of those two parties, I knew nothing of worldly life. This made it possible for me to grow up in this Christian environment without any preconceived notions or judgments.

Something occurred to me when I listened, paying attention to every word the preachers spoke. Along with accepting Jesus Christ as my savior, there were two primary directives that I must always hold with me: belief and faith. I must believe in God and have faith that through Jesus Christ, God would heal, shield, guide, prosper, sustain, refresh, and protect me as I went about my life. I understood that this was the foundation of everything all Christians believed. I, too, thought this to be true, but I wanted to see a miracle—something God would do.

Appeal For Confirmation

One Sunday, something that could have been considered a miracle happened at a church we visited once.

During the service, the pastor and others stood over someone with a disability and prayed. They often prayed for healing without delay. This person had used a wheelchair for many years. But after they prayed for him, he stood up from the wheelchair and walked away. The congregation erupted in praise for what they had just witnessed.

Seeing this miracle made new believers of some and strengthened others' faith, yet a few remained perceptively skeptical. Other instances occurred at various churches when people prayed over someone and the person claimed to have been healed. In most cases, there were no visible signs of healing; however, I could only accept that they had been healed and be happy for them.

Besides being adopted by my parents, at this point, nothing significant had happened to me personally that I could attribute directly to God. I did know that God kept my parents working with stable employment; to me, we lived comfortably. Reasonably blessed, my parents supplied every-thing we required, and I can confidently say I needed nothing.

We even traveled out of state on vacation several times; Niagara Falls was a favorite destination. We also visited amusement parks often, which I looked forward to every year. Once, Mom told me of a time when we struggled, eating oatmeal every day. She told me that when they made it through that trouble, everything necessary for our family to survive and thrive was a gift from God.

As a child of two preachers, I learned to pray purpose-fully by listening to my parents and others. My parents often prayed for those in helpless situations and aided those in need. If something unexpected happened to someone or someone became ill, they prayed together, asking God for help and healing. My mother's prayers were very passionate, and I could feel her emotion every time she prayed.

After earnest contemplation, I decided the time had come to pray and ask God not for help or healing but for certainty, so I prayed.

"Dear Heavenly Father, thank you for waking me this morning and for my health and home. I come to you today with a request. Please, Dear Heavenly Father, show me a sign that you are there and hear my prayers. In Jesus's name, I pray, Amen!"

An innocent request from one child among billions. Would he even hear me? Jesus did say, "Suffer little children, and forbid them not, to come unto me: for of such is the kingdom of heaven."—Matthew 19:14

Faultless Evidence

Sunlight glistened on the waves of the water as gentle breezes blew over it. Only wisps of clouds could be seen floating in the crystal-blue sky as the children's joyful voices filled the air. The adults stayed busy setting up the tables with the food prepared for the feast.

It was the day of our church picnic. We looked forward to the yearly outdoor gathering with much anticipation. Aside from all the food everyone brought, we played games, like volleyball and kickball, and explored the woods. And the reservoir lake was there to swim in. It was the main attraction.

At our first two picnics with this new church, my parents forbade me to go anywhere near the water; only the young adults could swim. After playing games and visiting other people's tables to taste their food, I began walking to ours. The noise from the lake drew my attention to the young adults splashing around and having fun. As I watched them, I thought to myself. *I am twelve now and learning to swim in the pool and at the YMCA. My parents might let me go in the water with them.*

The anticipation became too much to ignore. I couldn't watch anymore. I was ready to swim with the young adults in the lake, so I ran to our table to ask my parents. I asked, begged, and pleaded with them to let me go in. They became noticeably annoyed with my determination. Then, suddenly, to my absolute delight, they surrendered and allowed me to go swimming. The approval did, however, come with a stipulation: "Don't go too far out. Stay close to the beach."

I barely heard that part because as soon as they said yes, I was on my way to the water.

THIS WAS my first time running on a beach, so I wasn't prepared for how the sand moved when I stepped on it. Each step took extra effort, and my stride slowed as the sand slipped under my feet, but I kept going. Once I was there, the water splashed high with every step, making running farther out more difficult. So, to get through the water, I started high-stepping, which turned into a bounce as the water reached my waist.

Waves from the young adults splashing around pushed against me as I paused to watch them play. Some were swimming a little farther out, and as I watched them, I became curious. *What if I went farther into the water until it was up to my chest, like in the pool? Then, I could use what I have learned about swimming to swim back to play with the others.* I contemplated.

I looked around and didn't see anyone near me, and no one was blocking my way, so I decided to go for it. My bounces became shorter as the water got deeper and closer to my chest. I continued my bounce, bounce, bounce. Then the ground disappeared beneath me. Water rushed into my nose, mouth, and ears, covering my head completely. My arms and legs thrashed wildly, bringing me back to the top, but only briefly. My head went under again. Not willing to give up, I struggled harder to reach the surface again. I did, but only momentarily; the water entering my mouth muffled my cry for help as my body sank one last time.

I began drifting downward this third time with no fight left in me. My feet never touched the ground under the water again. I just drifted downward in a frozen state surrounded by nothing but water.

They say the third time you go under is when you start drowning because you've used all your energy struggling to stay afloat.

Looking up through the water at the sky moving farther away, I knew this was my end. My eyes began to close as I drifted farther down.

Then suddenly, a hand touched my shoulder and slid down my arm, holding it tight like a clamp. The person quickly pulled me back to the top, and I still remember what she said.

"Somebody, get this boy. He's scaring me!"

She walked me up to the beach and sent me on my way as I coughed and spit out water. She saved me! I don't think she ever knew how close to death's door I had come. As the shock of the situation started to diminish, it became clear to me that God had sent an angel to rescue me. Her name was Gloria, like the church song "Gloria in Excelsis Deo" ("Glory Be to God on High"). She was also the pastor's daughter, which itself held some significance.

Before I went out into the water, I looked around and saw no one near me. Somehow, Gloria saw me and could reach me in time. Yet it was a miracle for her to have been there at that exact moment.

"Glory be to God on high!" I told my parents, but they didn't believe me. That was a good thing. Who believed me didn't matter; I knew what had happened. Gloria was the guardian angel God sent to me that day. She saved me from certain death.

Promissory Agreement

"I asked, and God answered."—John 16:24.

Nothing could be more joyous than realizing that God heard my prayer and responded by sending an angel to rescue me from death. I was also relieved that God took no offense to my request for proof, which gave me a sense of value. This experience also taught me that God didn't judge me for that certain part of myself I kept subdued. Instead, God knew and embraced my faith and belief. The orchestration of the miracle left absolutely no doubts. It was definitive evidence, the physical and spiritual experience confirming that God was there. With this realization, I could not and will never question the existence of God.

My parents stopped going to parties and started attending church when I was five. From there to adolescence, my life consisted of church and spirituality, constantly. I grew up in the light of Christianity and was exposed to God's favor, which reassured me that if I had faith and believed, no matter my struggles in life, I could call on God, who would deliver me. It also ensured that when we honor the principles of spirituality, our lives will be healthy, long, and prosperous.

Fast approaching were the years when adulthood would take place, and preparations required attention. Most were routine, like advancing in school, meeting new people, and staying out of trouble. Yet there was a more significant preparation to undertake. It involved God and my desire to experience worldly ways.

Seeing and hearing about all the evil in the world over the years, I realized that spiritual security would be necessary if I was going to venture beyond the safety of my parents' home. That's why it was vital to know God would hear my prayers. And now it was time to ask God for His approval and protection.

~

"DEAR GOD, you know my desire, and I believe and have faith in your word that you will protect and guide me, even through the valley of the shadows of death. With no fear of evil, when I seek out worldly ways, I have faith that your staff will strengthen me in times of weakness, and I believe your rod will shield me from harm. In Jesus's name, I pray. Amen!"

My plea was, to me, another bold request of God. It took a while to receive the answer, but there was an answer. It came in random conversations, some at church and others at various times and places. Adults unaware of my request spoke from wisdom and knowledge of the world's ways, revealing strategies for managing and solving life's complexities. Receiving this knowledge from different people and aspects of life was an explicit confirmation that God acknowledged my request and would be with me no matter what happened or where life took me.

No one knew of my yearning; that was between God and me. The answer was a significant development, again confirming that my life mattered. There was, however, a two-part stipulation in this agreement. The first part was holding fast to the directives, the commandments, and my faith, regardless of any troubles and disadvantages. The second part of the stipulation would be revealed to me, and I would know what to do when the time came.

Without hesitation, I accepted, and everything was set and ready to go. The anticipation burned in me to live in the world, be my own boss, and do whatever I wanted. Getting through the school system and graduating was the next goal, and I was sure God would see me through. My parents told me that school would prepare me for living independently when my time came. Despite any difficulties that might arise, I would make every effort to ensure my schooling was consistent and successful. Failing and repeating were not options.

2

ACADEMIC PROCESSING

The Commencement

I faintly remember attending preschool at the City Community House at age four or five. I don't remember most of my time there, but I can remember the brick building, how it looked, and people coming and going. I can also recall one disturbing incident that happened to me there one day.

When the teacher finished reading the story, we ran to the toys and started playing. It was difficult to enjoy myself because our breakfast before the story made my stomach feel funny. It started cramping once, then again, and then a third time. The last time it cramped, my whole body jerked with the pulse of my stomach as it ejected my breakfast all over the toys.

One of the teachers ran over to me, snatched me up, and rushed me out of the room. I remember her calling my mother, who immediately came and picked me up. I never saw the others' reactions. I'm sure they were shocked. It was distressing to me because I remember it clearly. When I look back on it, even though I was technically still a baby, I humiliated myself in front of my classmates and teachers. After that traumatic experience, I have no memory of returning to preschool. I have only faint glimpses of kindergarten, so it must have been uneventful.

What I remember next is some of what happened at the elementary school on the hill.

Unforeseen Realizations

The laughing and yelling voices of hundreds of children echoed in the hallway as they headed to their classrooms. Everybody rushed past each other to beat the tardy bell before it rang. This elementary school was much larger than the Community House and had many more children.

Following my schedule was easy because most classes were on the same floor. After entering our classroom, we talked until the bell; then we sat at our desks and waited for the teacher to speak.

"Good morning, class," the teacher would say.

"Good morning, Teacher," we'd all reply together.

Every classroom had about twenty desks, and every room was usually full of students. This new school and all these kids offered countless opportunities to get to know different personalities and interact with them. *Making friends at this school shouldn't be hard at all*, I thought. As I learned new things daily and developed new friendships, this new school soon became comfortable.

That, ultimately, didn't apply to all my classes. I don't remember what I did in one class, but the teacher said something to me or did something that didn't seem right. I told my mother when I got home, and she became visibly and verbally upset, calling the teacher prejudiced. That was the first time I heard that word. I didn't know what it meant, so I asked.

She explained as much as she thought I would understand, and I did, for the most part. Some of what she told me had been on television, like when they held freedom marches in major cities around the country. I remember watching cartoons in the front room when a breaking news report interrupted my viewing. They showed people frantically running around this hotel with lights flashing from emergency vehicles parked around the building.

With emotional surprise in her voice, the reporter finally announced that Dr. Martin Luther King Jr. had been assassinated! I jumped up and ran to the kitchen to tell my mother. She ran back to the room with me to see the report. As we listened, she began crying, and I cried because of her emotion. Dr. King was a significant figure in our culture and called for peace among all people, but some saw him as a threat, so they killed him.

What was wrong with his message? I wondered.

I didn't understand.

MOST OF MY classes were tolerable, except for Spanish and math. English was my favorite class; I looked forward to attending it every day. At first, I couldn't read very well; the words seemed to run together, so I had to read slowly to comprehend. With extra effort, help from my teachers, and a pair of glasses from my mom, I improved over time. One class assignment I remember was when the teacher asked us to pick a stranger and create a short story about them to show how much we had learned. I chose the school crossing guard and got an A.

With my advancement to the next grade, my schedule of classes changed slightly. They put me in music class, which fit my interests perfectly, and I was thrilled when they added gym class right before recess. My grades in the other courses remained acceptable, and everything was going well, yet little did I know I was being observed my whole time there.

Every child in the school looked forward to going outside for recess. Sitting still in the last class before play-time was impossible. When the bell rang, everybody rushed out the classroom door. As my friends and I walked down onto the playground, another student ran up to us, stood right in front of me, and asked me a puzzling question.

"Why do you talk using those big words like White people?" he asked.

We were all speechless because my friends with me were White. Aside from not knowing the person and feeling the question was bold and abrupt, I couldn't answer because I didn't know that I spoke differently than anybody else. That's when I realized there was a difference between how I spoke and how people outside the church spoke. That confrontation ended without further incident, but others that were more substantially intense soon followed.

We lived several neighborhoods away from the school, so the long early morning walk was usually pleasant. I met up with other children along the way, and our group merged with others at the school crossing. When the crossing guard stepped into the street, holding his sign in the air, we all crossed and walked up the long driveway to the school building. That was my typical getting-to-school morning routine, but that pleasant routine was unexpectedly disrupted one day.

As a group of us stood at the crossing, talking and laughing about everything and waiting to cross the street, someone ran up behind me and punched me in the back of my head. It dazed me, and I fell into the crowd and onto the ground. When I looked to see who had hit me, to my surprise, it was Booker, who lived up the street from me. He rushed me when I stood up, and we fell back to the ground, wrestling, until the crossing guard broke up the fight.

I couldn't believe what had just happened. *Why did he jump on me and beat me up?* I wondered. After that initial attack, there were more confrontations, and eventually, he told me why.

He wanted my girlfriend.

She hadn't trusted me immediately; it took a while for her to let me walk her home from school. She didn't live far away, and her house was on my way home anyway. She was a beautiful Latina, and every guy wanted to make her his girlfriend, but she was mine. As she came to know me, she felt comfortable enough to invite me into her home to meet her family. They welcomed me openly; I had made it through the threshold.

Because she was the most admired girl in school, everybody knew her, and they knew I was with her. Out of all those who wanted to know her, the boy who had hit me was the only one bold enough to fight me to get her.

After he told me he wanted her and beat me up to get her, I stopped being her boyfriend. She was the prettiest girl in the school, but she was not pretty enough to get beaten up over. Later, the rumor around the school was that he tried but couldn't get her to be his girlfriend. She never spoke to or looked at me again.

EVENTUALLY, and unfortunately, others decided to express their dislike of me. They saw that I didn't know how to fight, and they knew most of my friends were White, so they decided to bully me every time they saw me. Once, as I was walking in the hallway to my next class, somebody walking behind me said they were going to beat me up after school. I didn't even know this person. *Why do they want to hurt me?* I wondered. I was sick the rest of the day. Scared and tired of getting beaten up, I sprung out of my seat when the last school bell rang, ran out of the classroom, and rushed to the nearest exit.

Most of the kids had just started leaving their classrooms and entering the hallway when I opened and ran out the front door. I jumped down the stairs, raced across the schoolyard to the adjoining street, and sprinted down that road to get as far away as possible. I figured that if someone still saw me and tried to follow, zigzagging through the streets might throw them off. My escape had to be fast, steady, and spontaneous. I ran as fast as possible, as I often had, through every random street that would get me home without any of them seeing me.

A student named Gray started confronting me inside the school because they could not catch me outside after school let out. One day, he followed me into my classroom and challenged me about one of my friends. He obviously didn't like my response because he attacked me. We ended up on the floor, tussling and rolling around, and with that, I had had enough of people bullying me all the time. When I finally worked my way on top of him, I beat him on the head repeatedly until the teacher pulled me off. The teacher scolded us. Then the guy went his way, and I went to my seat.

As it turned out, several people learned a lesson that day.

Nobody bullied me ever again. Surprisingly, Booker, who had assaulted me at the crossing, later became a good friend. Our partnership was unique because we were the two fastest runners in the school, so we had that in common. (Who was the fastest? I am not at liberty to divulge that information at this time.) Either way, Booker started inviting me to his house after school to visit and play; he turned out to be nice, and we became close. It was interesting to see how standing up for myself changed how others treated me.

Now that comfort had been restored, I didn't expect any distractions from my lessons or anybody trying to stop me from hanging out with whomever I wanted. My friends became more relaxed, and certain people I might have seen a few times around school became new friends. But upon meeting one new friend, Bo, that part of me that was to remain subdued became very intrigued.

We shared a bond of fun, laughter, and appreciation for each other's personality. We started hanging out often. Bo also lived near the school, only one block from my former girlfriend's house. I walked past his home twice daily, and we often walked together after school since it was on my way home.

When my new friend invited me into the house for the first time, I saw a Ping-Pong table in the basement. That was another of my favorite games that we played in the building at the park. I sometimes stopped by after school or visited on another day to play because I was determined to win at least one game. Bo was a superb Ping-Pong player; he'd learned the game by playing with his dad. Bo was quick and precise. His serve was what I liked the most, and I stole it and used it against my future competitors. Playing with Bo eventually improved my game and brought us closer.

One day after school, we went to Bo's house to play. As we whacked the plastic ball back and forth across the table, talking and laughing about everything, he said something that distracted me. At the same time, he hit the ball, and I had to go pick it up. When I bent over, he ran up to me and hit my backside with his paddle. Then he took off running with me right behind him, trying to smack his backside in return.

I took that playfulness as a sign that he had become comfortable enough with me to show that he acknowledged my attraction. He ducked under the table and ran around the furnace with me in close pursuit. I almost caught hold of his belt. On our third lap around the basement, when I'd almost caught him again, his father, who was just getting home from work, entered the side door. He immediately came to the basement because he heard the noise. He scolded us and then sent me on my way. After that, I was allowed to visit and play only in the yard. Bo and I never got to play Ping-Pong again, and my attraction returned to subdued.

WHEN I REACHED my final year at the school on the hill, advancing to junior high school was constantly on my mind. The city had several districts and junior high schools, so only some students in our school would go to the same junior high school. The district I lived in meant I would be attending the suburban valley junior high school.

One week before grade school graduation, excitement

about the ceremony was high. Everybody seemed to be in the happiest of moods. Cheerful voices filled the lunchroom as we conversed with excitement about graduating and going to another school. When my friends and I finished our meals, we headed for the door to the playground. Now outside, we had started to cross the driveway between the school and the playground when we saw people running in all directions.

Confused, I looked around and saw someone running toward us. The guy kept coming, and as he got closer, it became evident he was looking at me. Frozen in place, I quickly turned to see the hectic scene around us. I didn't know what to do. Rapidly turning back to the guy, I realized it was too late for me to move. He was there.

He punched me in the head and stomach and continued hitting me until I started running. I ran from the back of the school to the side, leaving him behind. When I started running across the grass, I saw other people getting chased and beaten in front of the school. I avoided another attacker by dodging his advance and escaped without getting jumped on again. I walked home in a roundabout direction once I was in the clear.

What was interesting about the fight was that Black kids were beating up other Black kids, and that appeared strange to me. Later, when I mentioned it to someone, they told me that they called the incident "the rumble." That's when a bunch of Black kids from the junior high schools came to the grade school on the hill to warn the Black sixth-graders that when they graduated and went to the suburban valley middle school, they were not to make friends with the White kids.

It was difficult for me to grasp how much it meant for Black kids not to mix with White kids or why interacting only with our own kind was so important. The Black community's tragic history, like Dr. King's assassination, was, I believe, significant to why they felt that way. While I experienced no adversities with my White schoolmates, it would be a challenge for me to navigate such conditions if they were to arise.

No other incidents occurred after the rumble, and graduation was a success. There was now, however, a shadow over the excitement of going to the new school. Because of the rumble, I didn't know what to expect.

Regardless of the Influence

Our neighborhood was far from the junior high school, but it wasn't far enough for them to bus me to the school. It had to be a two-and-a-half-mile walk to and from that school every day, but it wasn't far enough for me to ride the bus. I still think they could have bused me. That was a long walk, especially for a child.

The newly built school, which stood on a substantial part of the property, had its classrooms spread out on two floors. The complex spanned four city blocks, encompassing a school lawn, a regulation-size running track, and a soccer.

Upon arriving, I immediately noticed the overall ethnicity of the student body walking into the school. I was surprised; I expected to see more of my kind there, at least the ones who came to beat us up. There appeared to be so few of us that it wasn't often that we saw one another. I wouldn't have remembered the one who had jumped me anyway. Almost all the teachers were White; only a few had my skin color, and I was in one of those teachers' classes.

ONE DAY, an incident occurred in one class with a teacher who did not look like me. The students in the room weren't paying attention to the teacher as he wrote on the chalkboard and lectured us about the subject. Spitballs flew, plastering themselves on the sides of people's faces. Wadded-up paper balls bounced off people's heads, and one rolled to the front of the room. We were having fun. That is, until the teacher saw the paper wad, turned around, and caught me, of all people, throwing one at a classmate.

He ordered the class to quiet down and demanded that I leave immediately and stand in the hallway to wait for him. *Why did this teacher have to catch me?* I wondered. He was known around the school as a stern, no-nonsense teacher with a slugger swing. Getting paddled by him was something not soon forgotten.

My insides shook as I stood in the hallway, listening to the echoes of the voices coming from the other classrooms. I knew what was getting ready to happen to me, so I tried to prepare mentally.

My heart dropped when the teacher opened the door and came out into the hallway with the paddle. He had the one with the holes in it—the punisher. He told me to walk up to him, turn around, and bend over. My whole body was shaking with fear. I could see the teacher behind me through my legs, and I saw what he did. Like he was getting ready to swing a baseball bat, he reared back on one foot with his hand held high behind him. Then he swung the paddle as hard as he could into my backside.

I jumped up, landed about two feet away, and started running up and down the hallway, crying. That teacher hurt me badly, and he wanted to hit me three times. But I couldn't take any more. He made me return to the classroom and wanted me to sit in my seat, but I couldn't because of the pain. So he sent me to the office to ask them if I could go home.

As soon as I got home, I told my mother what he had done to me. She seemed more highly disturbed this time. After she reassured me that she would take care of it, the teacher hardly looked at me when I returned to his class.

The opposite of that event was when one of my teachers offered to give me a pet. You can't imagine my surprise when she asked me if I liked cats. A White teacher was offering me one of her kittens for free. I was amazed that she thought that much of me. We always had a pet in our house growing up, dogs and cats alike. We always had one or both, and I loved them. When my parents heard this, they were skeptical at first but saw my eagerness and agreed. The next day, I told the teacher they said yes.

She gave me a beautiful Siamese kitten, a precious little thing. Aside from telling me to take loving care of it, the teacher asked me to do something for her. She asked me to call him "Quickly," and I thought that was a unique name, so I honored her request. When my friends found out I had a Siamese cat, they all came to see my Quickly. Apart from what my parents did for me, giving me that cat was the most thoughtful thing anybody had done for me.

I JOINED the track team and loved running around the track, racing the other kids, and showing off my speed. When a track meet started, whatever the race was, the coach picked whoever specialized in that race. My strength was in the one-hundred-yard dash and the two-twenty-yard dash, and I even won a few races. Coach tried me on the hurdles, but my legs were too short to clear them. It didn't end well.

On my way to the track one day, I looked over to the field where they practiced soccer, and it looked like what they were doing was fun. Everybody was running around and kicking the ball. And trying to get it in the net looked challenging. I knew I could do that and wanted to try, but no kids like me were playing. Managing to suppress my urge to walk over and ask if I could play, I turned my attention to the track and continued walking there. In the back of my mind, I remembered the warning. This showed it did affect me; I didn't want to be the only one playing with them.

It became apparent, though, that the threat was a deception because most of the kids in the school were White. How could someone not make White friends when the school was full of them? As I said, very few of my ethnicity were in the school, and we hardly ever saw each other. A classroom would have one like me, none like me, or two like me, but never more than three. Sometimes, in passing, we might see each other in the hallways, but only sometimes. We lived so spread out that only four or three walked home together, and out of my group, I lived the farthest away from school.

❧

WINTERS WERE severe back in the day, and our school districts seldom granted snow days. This winter day was no exception. We received no news announcements or phone calls regarding the situation. Unfortunately, that meant I had to go to school regardless of how much snow was on the ground, and it didn't matter how hard it was snowing.

Mom helped me put on my boots and tightened my coat

so the wind couldn't get in. I put on my hat and mittens, and she sent me on my way.

When I stepped off the porch, the snow had already drifted high, making it difficult to walk. Snowflakes flew in my face with the force of the wind, causing me to lower my hood. The wind blew so hard at times that I had to bend over to fight through it.

The storm never let up, but I continued walking through it for a mile and a half to get to my school, which wasn't far enough away to ride the bus. When I arrived, I was almost frozen. I opened the door, and a wall of heat hit me in my face. I stomped to get some of the snow off, and as I continued walking, I was immediately met by a teacher.

"Oh, poor baby," she said as she brushed the snow off me. She later told me I looked like a little snowman; even my eyebrows and long eyelashes were covered with snow. As old as the story may sound, it is true: I walked over a mile in a snowstorm to get to my school.

THE REST of my time at the school in the valley was uneventful. Although, an unrelated peer event occurred during that time that broadened my horizons.

My friend Susie, who lived diagonally from our house on the corner—saw me out playing one day. She called me over to the dead-end street, and we walked down to the barrier where the park began.

When we arrived, she asked me if I wanted to get high. I knew what she meant, but I wasn't expecting her to ask that. My face must have shown my surprise, so she asked again with a big smile, "Do you want to smoke a joint?"

"Yes," I answered curiously, in anticipation of what would happen next.

She looked around, then took a joint out and lit it.

That was my first time smoking marijuana, so I did cough hard, but after that, I loved it! We continued smoking the strange-looking little cigarette, my brain started floating, and my body relaxed. It gave me a lightweight feeling and produced a carefree state of mind. Eventually, I found everything we talked about funny. We laughed about everything.

Another significant event during that time was when my parents told me there was a problem with our house that they couldn't fix, so we had to move. Moving got my attention for several reasons. Most importantly, it meant we would have to leave the neighborhood to live in a new one we didn't know anything about. It also meant that my sister, brother, and I had to leave our schools to attend different ones. This surprised me. I wasn't prepared for something as significant as this.

I liked our house and didn't want to leave it. I enjoyed my neighborhood friends and didn't want to leave them. Leaving the valley school meant leaving the friends I had just made. *What will the new neighborhood and the kids living there be like?* I wondered. All these things came to mind, yet no matter how much I liked the house and didn't want to leave my friends, I couldn't stay, so the move won by default.

Cultural Event

We moved to the Heights into a much smaller house than our two-story house on the corner lot. I wouldn't say I liked it initially, but it soon grew on me. The style of the homes in this neighborhood didn't differ much; they all were similar in build and features. Our house was built on a slight hill close to the end of a quiet dead-end residential street. All the bedrooms and other rooms were on one main floor, with a basement below.

The backyard was tiny compared to the one we moved from, but it wasn't so small that the pool couldn't fit; my dad had it up in no time. Cutting the grass at this house would be a breeze. The front yard was small too. Our old house had a dilapidated garage that my dad had torn down shortly after we moved in. This new house had a garage in perfect condition, and that's where my dad parked his small four-speed stick shift car that no longer worked; he said it was called an Opal. Whenever my parents left the house, I ran to the garage and played in it. I must have ridden in the Opal or another stick shift before because I remembered how Dad shifted the gears and when he pressed the gas, brake, and clutch. So, with sound effects and all, I drove that little Opal to wherever my imagination took me.

THE TIME HAD FINALLY ARRIVED: the first day of my second year in junior high school at a different school. My siblings, who were still in grade school, walked only two blocks to theirs, but mine was much farther away. Almost every street in the Heights had a hill at some point, so walking to school was physically challenging at first. Even though it wasn't so far, this school seemed miles away, primarily because of those hills. And they still wouldn't let me ride the bus.

With its many windows, this big brick junior high school stood stately between corporate office buildings, parking lots, the county library, and a car dealership. Surrounded by a boulder wall, its front yard rose above street level. Steps made in the wall led up to the long sidewalk that led to the front door, which is how some students entered.

The running track was behind the school on the other side of an access road. My route brought me out of the hills to that road, and as I walked closer to the back of the school, I saw that everybody else walking looked like me. All the students coming into this school had my skin color.

I had hoped I would be around more kids who looked like me at my new school, but I wasn't expecting the whole school to be this way. Only in the church had I been around large groups of my kind. That happened once a year, on Sundays, and sometimes during the week. Being around hundreds of kids like me in the same building daily was an unexpected experience, especially after coming from the suburban valley middle school.

Upon receiving my class assignments, I headed off to my first class. I noticed a few other ethnic students walking through the halls alone. I couldn't help but wonder how they felt being surrounded by people of my kind all day long. Did they feel uncomfortable in any way? *Surely*, I thought, *they must have a group of friends to hang out with.*

LEARNING that someone else in this school ran faster than me was a surprising disappointment.

There were really two people who could run faster than I could, which made it doubly difficult to accept. I was amazed at how fast they could run. One was short with muscles everywhere, and the other was taller and slender with bowlegs. When we raced in practice, I just could not beat their times, but I continued to try diligently. I did manage to hold on to the position of third fastest in the school, and with my participation, we did win several track meets.

But at one track meet, we were not so fortunate. The whistle signaled for my race to begin, and all runners stepped up to their marked lanes. We all crouched in our starting position, and the countdown started.

"On your mark. Get set. Go!"

We took off running down the straightaway and then around the curve. One runner from another team pulled out in front as we sprinted down the other straightaway, and when we came out of the last bend, no matter how hard we tried, he beat all of us to the finish line.

I was devastated because I had lost by so much. It wasn't even close. We lost other races that day as well and ultimately lost the meet.

Muscles, Legs, and I were, nevertheless, the fastest kids in the school. We still won many meets, so my name and reputation started getting around. While I developed team and teammate cohesion, other friendships began to take shape with some of the kids in my classes. Eventually, I came to know my neighbors, who attended the school and happened to live on the next street. The more we got to know each other, the more we had in common.

As teenagers, my new friends and I always spent time together and ventured everywhere together in the Heights. We walked to and from school every day, and sometimes, we walked all the way down to the valley to visit. I'll tell you why in a minute.

One of us stood out as a unique, headstrong personality with an unusual laugh and manner of joking. He often got in trouble with his parents, us, and others. He was, on the other hand, very entertaining to have around at parties.

Still, inclusive of his friendship, we formed a tight social circle, attending parties and indulging in marijuana use together. This habit mirrored my initial experience in the neighborhood—that first time with Susie on the dead-end street, a feeling I hadn't forgotten. Now, that same euphoria was a near-daily occurrence.

Sometimes, when our supply ran out and no one in the Heights had anything to sell, we periodically walked about four miles to the valley, even during winter, to get our marijuana. Usually, two of us made the trip, but whichever one walked with me, I struggled to keep up. They were taller than me, and with their long strides, one of their steps seemed like two of mine. We walked along the snow-covered main street and several side streets, with the wind blowing frigid temperatures in our faces, because we were determined to reach our objective at all costs. It was similar to when I walked through that snowstorm to get to the valley school.

When it was time to go to a party, we smoked on the way there, while there, and on the way back. Even when we didn't go to parties, we smoked all the time. At that age, I had just started drinking; it was a part of being with the popular crowd, as was smoking marijuana daily. When we visited each other's homes, we didn't smoke. We knew better. The parents of one of my friends knew he smoked but didn't allow it in the house. I don't know if the other friend's parents knew or not. My parents didn't know I smoked, I don't think, although they did ask me once, and I denied it.

The four of us always found things to do; we never had a dull day together. Unfortunately, one day, our headstrong partner moved away from the neighborhood. We never saw him again except at one party in the valley. That left the three of us, the GY Heights Trio, who were always together, doing what we did—getting high and partying. Of all the people I met at that school, I miss those three the most.

❧

WRESTLING class was an organized version of the way my friends and I had played together in the old neighborhood, like when my best friend almost broke my back. Most wrestlers were good, but I held my own when the time came. Placed in the lightweight category, I wrestled others my size, which gave me an advantage after the experience of wrestling with my friends, who were all bigger than me. As my skills progressed, I became more successful with each win. The coach wanted me to start practicing with some of the veteran wrestlers on the team, so he picked the person he wanted me to wrestle with at the start of one practice.

His choice of people surprised me because it was someone my attraction had come to admire. Whenever we hung out together, we shared in playful conversation and joked around with each other. During practice, he was sometimes unusually playful but managed to win his matches.

We both got into our starting positions, with me on my hands and knees and him on one knee, holding on to me.

Before the referee said go, he took his arm from around my waist and used that hand to grab me between my legs. I jumped up immediately. That shocked me.

The match was over before it started. *To do what he did,* I thought, *he either admires me or it was a strategy. Or was it both?* Either way, the idea of us wrestling together after that public and unexpected gesture made me apprehensive. My attraction returned to subdued.

BEING in this enclosed environment with hundreds of my kind was initially an overwhelming experience, although it was enlightening as well. It allowed me to learn more about my culture and how others like me lived. As far as I remember, there were only a few fights at this school, and most students seemed to get along harmoniously. We were known as a proud school with successful academics and winning sports teams.

During my time at Brick Junior High School, I became a recognizable figure, surrounded by peers who shared my skin color and features and possessed unique personalities. Interacting with them tested my resolve, especially as I grew closer to some who shared similar interests. However, due to our busy schedules and individual activities, our relationships never progressed beyond cordial acquaintanceships. As my second year concluded, I not only graduated but also gained insight into the lives of those who were like me but didn't attend church.

With this advancement, the administration offered me a choice of two high schools to attend after graduation. The first was the high school in my district, well-known for its sports and specialty courses. The second was a vocational trade high school located downtown at the city's center, which offered state certifications upon course completion. I chose the trade high school because a certification almost guaranteed employment. Advanced Arts would be my course study, considering my artistic background, and I would follow in my dad's footsteps.

Occupational Development

Every bump in the road shook the entire metal structure, creating startling sounds from the loosened doors and windows. The engine's roar stifled most other sounds, and no one talked as the large steel vehicle trembled its way through the city. We rode through the neighborhoods, most of which I had never seen before, and then we headed downtown.

Yes, I was finally riding a bus to school, but it wasn't a school bus. Of course, they still couldn't do that. It was the city bus, but a bus, nevertheless. Kids from everywhere came to the Center City High School to learn a trade and participate in other classes and sports, so many of them also caught the bus.

Nestled between the children's hospital, parking lots, and office buildings, this seven-story brick structure stood ominously apart from the other facilities in the area. When the bus stopped at the side of the school, I hopped out and walked toward the building. As more students arrived, a crowd formed at the door. This student body was not overly populated with one ethnicity, like my other schools, so I thought that fitting in should be effortless.

An energy filled the hallways as students scurried, trying to find their homerooms. Once there, the students and teachers followed the same routine as in other classrooms. The bell rang, the teacher greeted the students, and the students responded together, "Good Morning, Teacher," though sometimes not so enthusiastically.

Looking around the room at wall hangings and books made it clear that this class would be more than coloring or scribbling on a piece of paper. The Advanced Arts course covered several aspects of the art culture, from the Renaissance to modern-day advertising. We were to learn everything about the art world and become knowledgeable, skilled, and able to create our own artistic originals.

The chance to study photography was a surprising delight; I didn't expect it to be a part of the class. We were all given a camera with instructions on how to use it. Afterward, the teacher took us into the darkroom to show us how to develop our film. Watching the process of what for me had been a mystery for so long was fascinating. As we watched, small, faded objects grew darker, and items began to appear, forming solid images from the white paper background. Soon, the entire page displayed what someone had captured and frozen in time to be viewed by future admirers.

YOU ALREADY KNOW the school choir would be one of my classes. Our voices blended into perfect harmony whenever we opened our mouths, and that's because the choir director was superb at her job. Short in stature, she was a professional of the highest caliber. We practiced meticulously during class and sometimes after school, and she left nothing unaddressed. She explained how each voice range worked and taught us how they fit together; the bass section was the foundation for the rest. She told me my voice was baritone and put me in the bass section.

Baritones have separate parts in some songs, but we usually sang along with the bass section. One of my goals was to reach the bottom notes, as the true basses did, and I succeeded a few times. I could also sing into the second tenor range; I loved doing that most. So sometimes, as the choir sang when the tenors had a solo, I sang along with the tenors if the range wasn't too high.

My cousin, who was a second tenor, was one year ahead of me and also sang in the choir. We tried to stand close to each other when we could, sometimes singing along with each other's parts when in range, then switching back to ours as if nothing had ever happened. I thought it gave each part richness in a song's top or lower tones. He and I enjoyed harmonizing, and our voices sounded unique together. The music director even created a barbershop quartet with two other males, my cousin and me. She also created another group called The Madrigals, in which we sang together with a soprano and an alto.

Sometimes I smiled to myself while watching my cousin sing. He put a lot of emotion into it, periodically bouncing his big, curly, soft Afro as he nodded with a feeling or to a beat. My cousin was an entertaining, pleasant, joyful personality to be around. I don't remember ever seeing him angry about anything. He also lived in the Heights, and even though he was a year ahead of me, we still spent time together.

He and I also participated in two musical productions at school, one of which included the barbershop quartet. Our choir director, other teachers with similar experience, choreographers, production managers, and choir members collaborated to put on famous Broadway shows every year. Our first play was my initial exposure to the world of character expression in theater. Before this experience, I knew little of Broadway, so acting in an onstage play was a phenomenal event.

Despite being warned about the potential confusion it could cause for other actors delivering their lines, my cousin often improvised on stage, resulting in laughter from the audience. It rarely confused the other actors, who laughed along yet still spoke their lines on cue. Everybody had great fun together and eagerly anticipated the following year's production. Our families and friends were genuinely proud of us and spoke highly of the experience for many days to come.

AFTER CHOIR REHEARSAL ONE DAY, a friend and I were walking the hallway as we headed for the lunchroom. The building was so old that one whole section had been blocked off. We always wondered what they didn't want us to see behind the locked door, and one day, we decided to investigate. The door wasn't going to budge, but we thought a window around the side of the building might be open and we could get in that way. When we found one and climbed in, we couldn't believe our eyes when we dropped to the floor and looked around. It was an old auditorium that hadn't been used in years.

A layer of thick dust covered everything. The chairs, the stage, and even the wallpaper were faded by dust. Most windows had boards covering them, and wooden planks lay across some seats and around the stage. Cardboard boxes and other debris also lay about, as if the place had been under construction before they abandoned it. We walked across the stage, looking around at the ill repair of the audi-torium; it was heartbreaking. We walked back to center stage, looked out over the seats, paused, and then did what any kid would do—we yelled to hear our voices echo.

Not singing in that auditorium was a missed opportu-nity; I would have loved to have heard my choir sing there. A good friend of mine often says every disappointment is for a good. This old eyesore brick building had finally succumbed to old age's ravages; it was unsafe to accommodate so many students much longer. In this case, the good would be to practice in a brand-new choir room and sing in a brand-new auditorium at a brand-new school. That was okay with me; I had been through the switching-school-buildings thing before. Only this time, it was from an old building to a new one, not from a new one to an old one like when I moved from the suburban valley school to the brick school while attending junior high.

OUR BRAND-NEW high school was located near the university in the city center, near the old school; I just had to get off at a different stop and walk a short distance to get there. All the classrooms in this school occupied three floors and two-thirds of the building. The gym, choir room, and auditorium were at the east end of the structure. Outside, across from the auditorium entrance, was a parking lot where the kids who drove parked and sometimes went to get high.

Winding sidewalks led from adjoining streets through the manicured front lawn to the school's front entrance. Above the doorway, a white marble plaque, engraved with the school's name, Dimond City Center High School, was flanked by two white marble columns. Neatly trimmed bushes lined the front and side of the building, with dark mulch laid out under them. With its symmetrical design, it looked like a flawless diamond compared to the other buildings around it.

When we entered, the building smelled of freshness, and everything looked shiny new. We walked around in awe of the craftsmanship we saw; even the class bell sounded distinct. The hallway floors sparkled with a high-gloss shine, and hand railings ran along every wall. Big windows covered one side of each classroom, and glass panes bordered the doors to every room.

How they had designed the back of the school was interesting. The parking lot was at street level, but the two back doors entering the school were not because the building was built into a small hill. When we walked toward the school from the parking lot, two flights of stairs led down to a door to the bottom floor of the school. Another entrance was built on the lower platform's other side, creating a below-ground-level area where students could hang out between classes. Those who smoked cigarettes gathered there to smoke, so we called it The Smoke Pit.

We did smoke cigarettes in the pit, but we also smoked something else. We knew each other's class schedules, so we met in the pit and smoked our joints together when breaks came. Everybody knew somebody who got high in the pit. If someone needed to buy some, somebody in the pit always knew who was selling in the school. Usually, two or three people smoked in the pit at one time; sometimes, there were more, like this one snowy day in winter.

I'll never forget us being huddled near the secondary back door, trying to stay warm as the wind blew into the pit. Everybody pulled out their joints, all wrapped in assorted colors, and we all burst out laughing. It was the holiday season, and we all had presents for each other. As we passed around the joints, reefer smoke and the steam from our breath billowed around our heads like low-lying clouds. Everyone also seemed to have brought several types of marijuana. As we smoked, our gathering became even more festive as we talked and laughed about everything.

We were noticeably high and the only people in the pit

during the snowstorm. One of the teachers came to the door and told us to stop smoking and come in. When the door opened, a welcome rush of warm air hit my face, but the noise from all the students startled my high. All types of voices of every range and intensity echoed off every surface in the hall. It turned into a loud, muffled throbbing sound that distracted me momentarily, which caused a slight instability, and my feet stumbled as I stepped through the door.

As if nothing was wrong with me, I continued walking to my art class to sit in my private cubicle, out of sight of everybody. I hurried there because the white parts of my eyes turned bloodshot red every time I smoked. It didn't matter how little or how much; they always turned red. Because of my eyes, everybody in school, even some teachers, knew what I was doing. It didn't help that I probably smelled like it and always laughed at something.

My friend Trey and I smoked a joint in the pit before music class one day; he told me it was his first time getting high. We laughed from the pit all the way to the choir room. When we entered, he went to his section, and I went to mine, but we kept looking at each other and couldn't stop laughing. Everybody else quieted down when the teacher came out of her office to start class, but we kept laughing. The glare she gave me when I looked at her pierced right through me, wiping that smile off my face. It was a miracle that none of the teachers ever approached me about it or suspended me for smoking marijuana on school grounds.

EVEN THOUGH I smoked marijuana and cigarettes daily, it didn't inhibit my ability to sing. When the bell rang, every choir member headed for our new music room for practice.

When we entered the room, it was bright, beautiful, and huge, with risers along one wall for us to sit on and offices at the far end. The piano was stationed at the corner of the risers, and the rest of the room was open space.

Walking into this beautiful, newly constructed music room was fascinating. The way the room made our voices sound also captured our attention. It was designed with the acoustics of an auditorium in mind. When we practiced, we filled the room with a beautiful sound, and when we sang the last note of a song and stopped, the echo was purely harmonious.

One day, my music director surprised me and asked if I would like to participate in a unique music course at Case Western Reserve University. Intrigued, I eagerly listened as she explained that this course focused on classical music, and she expressed her desire to send me to the university to participate in the course.

We studied classical music in class, so everyone was familiar with it, but I never thought of myself as someone who could sing classical music. *What does my voice sound like, anyway?* I wondered. I didn't know how my voice sounded to other people. I didn't know how I sounded at all. I never heard myself outside myself.

One day, I took my tape recorder and taped myself talking and singing one of the songs from school. My jaw dropped when I played it back. When I heard it, I could not believe what was coming from my mouth. *Is that how I sound to others?* I thought. I sounded like a totally different person to myself. That would explain why some people encouraged me to sing, like my mom when she asked me to sing her favorite song.

My teacher contacted my parents, and Mom and Dad said I could study at the university. They made all the proper arrangements, and I was off to what could be considered prep school during summer break.

Nestled in a grassy enclave with wrought-iron fencing and giant shade trees, the historic Case Western Reserve University included three-story brick buildings ascending a slight hillside. When we drove onto the campus, the auditorium on the left stood apart from the other buildings in its design. After pulling up to the main building, we exited the car, greeted by the scent of freshly cut grass. We hugged, and I waved goodbye to my parents as I headed into the main building.

The office building lobby was busy with people walking in different directions. Kids from all over the region had come to attend this exclusive training. The check-in desk was straight ahead, and I made my way through the crowd. They assigned me to a room and gave me documents explaining the arrangements and the course study. *Is this really happening?* I wondered. It was like a dream come true, but a dream I'd never had or something that happens in movies. I was a senior in high school, and I was attending a college preparatory program at Case Western Reserve University.

Seeing all those bright personalities and friendly attitudes was a delightful experience. The inclusive treatment I received from everybody put me at ease. They sent me to the building where the guys would be housed. Each room on every floor had two students assigned to it, so the building was busy with activities. While I was settling into my room, my new roommate walked in. We spoke and briefly learned a little about each other; he was a friendly kid, which made our pairing comfortable.

We kids started getting to know each other when not in the confines of our training. We shared a common interest and had a collective purpose and goal to pursue. That's what made being around them so comfortable and made some of us comfortable with each other. Some of us quickly became friends and hung out together at every opportunity. Becoming acquainted with all these individuals in this environment was fun and exciting. It was also advantageous.

ONE DAY, my roommate asked me to follow him. We went behind our building and stood under a tree. From his pocket, he pulled out a joint and said, "Look!"

I was surprised that he managed to bring it into the school, but it didn't matter. Nodding in agreement, we began to smoke. As usual, my eyes turned red, and we laughed about everything. However, I hadn't considered the implications of being high around all the other kids, especially since it had been a while since I last got high.

Walking through the hallway was troublesome, with people running up and down the hall and from room to room. It didn't seem like anyone noticed that we were high as we walked to ours. When we finally got there, we closed the door and decided to stay out of sight for a while.

Now inside and shut away from the crowd, we talked, laughed, and started wrestling around with each other. We smoked a couple of times after that, but one time, when we went out, he said, "Come on. I want to show you something."

He said, "I'm going to blow you a gun. When you take it,

I will get behind you and grab and squeeze you. Do not let the smoke out until I let go."

Of course I said okay. I had given and taken guns before. The only difference here was the squeezing, which made me curious. He blew me the gun, got behind me, grabbed me, and squeezed me with all his might.

When he let go of me, I let go of the smoke and dropped to the ground like a wet rag. That was more than a blast; it blew me away. My ears were ringing, my vision was blurred, and my body was limp. It took a minute to recover from the effect. When I looked up at him, he smiled and laughed at me. I'll admit, I started laughing too. The whole purpose was to have me experience the ultimate high, which he succeeded in doing.

We continued to go out to our spot and smoke, giving each other guns, and he let me squeeze him, too, but I couldn't squeeze him as hard, so I'm sure he didn't experience the same effect. By this time, we had established a comfortable friendship, enough to play and wrestle with each other often. One day, being taller and weighing more than me, he pinned me down on the bed, holding my arms at the sides of my head with his knees.

We both knew where our playfulness was leading, and the difference in our ethnicity didn't matter. We were frozen in a moment of exhaustion, and it seemed like something was about to occur. But it didn't. The match ended abruptly; he told me why, and as he got off me, my attraction returned to subdued. Our friendship remained cordial, and we continued getting high together; we just didn't wrestle with each other anymore.

~

TWO OTHERS DREW MY ATTENTION, causing that part of me to remain aware. Their room was across the hall from mine. One was of my ethnicity, a friend made at the beginning of our stay. I approached the person carefully and respectfully and asked if I could express my attraction to them. They took no offense but said they did not participate in the activity. I understood and accepted that. It was reassuring that we maintained a friendship after I approached them.

The other person was their roommate, who was of the other ethnicity. To my surprise, they had no problem participating in the expression when asked. Our encounters, subtle at first, grew in frequency—once while the other roommate was sleeping. Well, we thought they were asleep, but they brought it up to me the following day as we walked to breakfast.

"Were you in my room last night," they asked. I answered truthfully, and they continued, saying, "I thought I was dreaming, but it was real."

It was uncomfortable being around them after doing what we did, thinking they were asleep when they weren't. It was disrespectful and embarrassing, and I felt bad that it happened. I apologized from the depths of my humility. To my relief, our friendship remained unchanged because of their accepting spirit; they even invited me to visit them when we finished the course.

The other roommate and I stopped seeing each other after that. None of us ever spoke to another person of what happened, as far as I knew. Not that it would have mattered. We were all at the age of discovery, and I was positive we weren't the only ones in that building expressing to others.

After that, I put all my attention on the music. I could not let that happen again; my attraction returned to subdued.

THE REHEARSALS COULD HAVE BEEN CONSIDERED GRUELING if they weren't so much fun. We sat in classes and learned our parts separately, in small groups, with the entire choir, and eventually with the full orchestra until we sounded supreme. During the process of this once-in-a-lifetime opportunity, another unexpected happening occurred.

One of the instructors shocked me by asking me to sing a solo. There were hundreds of kids attending this course, and the instructor asked me to sing a solo. My mind paused to assess the importance of his request; my eyes grew wide with eagerness as my mind produced visions of renowned success. Nodding and saying yes at the same time, I accepted and thanked him for the opportunity. After our brief meeting, the musician gave me the song I would sing, and my formal one-on-one classical voice training began.

Everyone headed to the auditorium to rehearse the day before the concert; most had already arrived when I entered the building. On instinct, I looked into my folder and saw that my music wasn't there. I found the instructor and told him I had left my music in my room and would be right back. I ran out of the auditorium to my building and my room. I grabbed my music off my bed, then ran out of the room and back to the hall. It took about eight minutes for me to finally walk back through the door. They had already begun rehearsing.

There wasn't any more time to finish catching my breath; they had arrived at the part when my solo would be sung. Worried about trying to sing when out of breath, I looked at the instructor, hoping they could delay my solo until I could breathe. Shaking his head, he declined to give me time and directed me to the microphone.

The orchestra played the introduction, and I started singing. It took a lot of effort to sing that song while hardly able to breathe, but I did it. I sang the whole song without error. After rehearsal, the instructor told me that being out of breath caused me to breathe deeply, using my diaphragm to support my voice. He said, "Your breathing and diaphragm are what you want to remember and use every time you sing."

When concert day arrived, we were all anxious and giddy with anticipation. When the time came, we gathered behind the stage curtains, where the orchestra awaited their opening. Peeking through the curtains, we saw that the auditorium was packed. It looked like everyone's families and friends had come to hear us perform.

The orchestra began playing the introduction, the curtains opened, and we began to sing. When our voices joined the orchestra, the auditorium was filled with a spectacular sound. I cannot adequately express what it was like standing amidst all those voices as they sang and the orchestral instruments as they played. Performing my solo backed by the full orchestra was a surreal, incredible experience. Never would the chance to take part in making such beautiful music have happened if not for my music director. Additionally, it was an opportunity of the highest honor and a distinct privilege to sing for an audience of classical music enthusiasts.

~

THOUGH NOT CLASSICAL, my high school choir always sounded fantastic when we performed. Aside from our scheduled engagements, we also took part in competitions. One was the yearly state music competition held in various cities statewide. One year, our city college hosted the contest, so most events were within walking distance from our school. They even used our beautiful choir room as one of the performance locations. We walked to the college performing arts hall to participate in our events, and after our little break, we hurried in and joined our groups.

Countless voices filled the enormous auditorium with thunderous chatter from everybody talking and walking in all directions as they tried to reach their destinations. Many had begun taking their seats as we walked by, and the competition participants gathered behind the curtains on stage. We were told the order in which we were to perform, and my spot was lucky number three. I had hoped it wouldn't have been that soon, but at least I wasn't first.

This lineup was for the men's solo competition, in which my choir director had entered my name. From joining the children's choir to this moment, I had never imagined I would compete for best male singer against other male singers statewide. The pressure was on. I listened closely as the first two participants sang. Both sounded exceptional as they rendered their solos, and the audience responded with cheerful applause.

My introduction sounded more beautiful than ever as I walked to the center stage microphone, breathing deeply to prepare and manage my nerves. On cue, my mouth opened, and my voice attacked the first note with the energy of breath and diaphragm control. My delivery was passionate and expressive; my interpretation of the music was compelling. The audience responded, and I hurried off stage, hoping I had done well enough.

The following person also sounded great. To me, when it was over, we all sounded incredible. We lined up across the stage as the presenter walked to the microphone with the envelope. He said a few words to get the audience's attention as he opened it.

"And the winner of the state music competition male solo award goes to ..."

I won! He said my name! I actually won! It felt unreal, like a dream. Looking at the audience clapping and cheering for me eliminated any doubts. It made it clear that my pitch-perfect musical ability was indeed a gift given by God.

It took several days for what happened to sink in, but I don't think it ever really did. Not all of it, not entirely. My whole family expressed their happiness for me; some were surprised but still happy. Mom and Dad were the happiest for me and were most proud. Overcome with humility and a deep sense of honor, I found that sharing these exceptionally rare and privileged accomplishments with my parents was a profoundly emotional experience.

Their son had achieved something significant and noteworthy, something everyone could admire about the child they had raised. This accomplishment and this award did extend beyond me. It was a direct result of the contributions of others along the way. They obviously saw something and heard something they felt deserved nurturing, investing in, and taking a chance on. It was my honor not to let them down.

More personalities began entering my life during my activities, classes, and final grade-level advancement. As seniors, we knew most of the kids at the junior level, having become friends with some the year before. One junior stood apart from most with the sweetest disposition, joyful laugh, and cheerful smile. Kind and attentive, Janice often expressed how much she cared for others. We both sang in the school choir, and she was also a member at a church across the city; that was something else we had in common.

Janice was distinguished from her peers, radiated refinement, and we often sought solitude away from the crowd. Our discussions seldom touched upon my artist friend; instead, we engaged in lighthearted conversations about church and activities at the school.

As I got to know her, I also became close friends with another person with whom I shared three school activities. When we met, I was a junior, and Trey had just come to the school as a sophomore. The dormant interest was awakened again. We both played soccer, sang in the choir, and attended the Advanced Arts class. He was the one who smoked the joint for the first time. He was a talented artist who could create or recreate anything from memory or visual reference. His finished work was always impressive.

We often rode our bicycles for miles to and from each other's homes and even to soccer practice. Yes, the opportunity to play soccer presented itself, and I signed up immediately. Having such a close friend playing on the soccer field with me made me slightly self-conscious; I just needed to be sure not to show favoritism or my attraction in front of the others. I don't think anyone knew or suspected how close we were. That's how it was at first, but many in the school learned differently as time progressed.

Our reputations as accomplished students and, regrettably, marijuana smokers, preceded us throughout the school. Unbeknownst to me, I held a high-profile status, oblivious to how other perceived me.

Plans had begun for the school prom. It was a central topic of many discussions around the school. Everyone knew about high school proms—the dancing, the parties, and who attended with whom. The person someone took to the dance seemed to be a primary focus; it symbolized status and foresight. I believed I had proved worthy of attending the prom, so I approached Mom and Dad to ask them. There was only one person to take, and my parents approved; they even told me I could use their car to take Janice to the prom.

Pulling up to her house in my dad's Cadillac, I felt proud to be there for her. I went through all the formalities as a gentleman would do, and then we proceeded to the party. No way was I going to this party not high; I even drank a little while there. It was social; my date sipped some also. Halfway through, I excused myself, stepped outside to smoke another joint, and returned inside feeling mellow. We danced, laughed, and talked about everything. We had a ball.

Couples began to leave as the festive energy lessened. The party had ended. On our way to the car, Janice expressed how much she had enjoyed herself and thanked me for bringing her. The experience was enjoyable; my feelings were in a happy place. We sat in the car and talked for a few minutes; then, she popped the question. She wanted to kiss me, and I said okay. When our lips touched, I was immediately reminded of when my rough-and-tumble girlfriend had done the same. It didn't feel like it had been made out to be; it did not feel comfortable to me.

Pulling away carefully to avoid insulting her, I sat up straight in my seat and prepared to complete the night. When we arrived at her home, I performed the formalities and bid her goodbye as any gentleman would. So, the prom was a success except for the very last part. I never saw Janice again outside school or after graduating. We spoke to each other once over the phone, and she invited me to her church, but I didn't go. She was a lovely young lady, but my essence was uncomfortable with even the possibility of expressing myself that way.

My artist friend, Trey, and I were still seeing each other during my last year and, yes, around the time of the prom. I mentioned the prom and what my date had done, but Trey didn't seem to mind because our bond had been sealed with actions. There was nothing I could do to limit my attraction; my desire could not be controlled. We showed the same interest as our coupling strengthened until, one day, we declared our standing to each other. We agreed to be monogamous; my attraction fully surrendered.

EVERY DIAMOND CITY Center High School senior was prepared to receive their public school diploma. It proved that we had gained the knowledge necessary to go out into the world and live productive lives. Excitement filled the classrooms and hallways during the days leading up to graduation.

On commencement day, our caps knocked into each other as we shuffled around excitedly backstage. Some put on their gowns hurriedly, and others shifted them for a better fit when soft music began playing. We all lined up, walked in unison to the chairs, and sat in our assigned seats.

At the start of the ceremony, they announced the students' club accomplishments and those of students separately. I won the Most Accomplished School Musician Award. Again, I had received another recognition because I shared my God-given gift with others. What made it even better was that I had a whole lot of fun doing it. The speaker continued, mentioning all the other class achievements that year.

Finally, the formal segment of the ceremony began, marking a significant moment for me. A feeling of empowerment swelled within me as I made my way across the stage, fully aware of my accomplishment. I was immensely proud and intellectually relieved. Yet I must give all the credit to God, who I know brought me through without failure as a result of my unwavering belief and strong faith. This foundation would prove indispensable as I embarked on my journey into the ways of the world.

THE YEAR WAS 1977, and my academic instruction was complete, leaving me free to do whatever I wanted as a young adult. I chose to hang out with my cousin when I should have been looking for a job, but a job was the furthest thing from my mind. I wanted to continue celebrating my accomplishments and be free for a while. My cousin and I visited everybody he knew in the Heights to party and have fun. He was the stand-out guy at any social event, with his cheerful personality and natural charm; everyone liked having him around.

After about a month of drifting around the neighborhoods, getting high and drunk, I grew bored of the repetition. My first search for a job requiring my qualifications was unsuccessful, making me slightly depressed, so I stopped looking. One day, my cousin unexpectedly told me that one of our cousins was a US Army recruiter and that he wanted to talk to the male cousins together. The first thought that came to my mind about the army was a creation of my attraction; the second was a glimpse of the

Earth. In the army, I would get the chance to travel farther and meet more people than I could imagine. This was the opportunity of a lifetime, which I could not refuse.

We met with him, and he explained all the benefits of joining, even the possibility of military conflicts. Thankfully, we were in peacetime. *Hopefully, they won't start a war any time soon*, I thought.

Three of us decided to go in. My parents didn't know about the meeting, but I told them about it when I returned home.

"Are you sure that's what you want to do?" That was the question my mother asked me, and I will never forget it.

"Yes," I told her. "I want to join."

They both said, "Okay, if that's what you want to do."

And I was on my way.

Something was overlooked in the days of getting high, in the drunkenness, and during the exciting recruitment process. I did not give much attention to my artist friend, Trey, for reasons I can't recall; we subsequently drifted apart. Since we no longer interacted, remembering the details is difficult. Did I tell Trey I was joining? I have no memory of a conversation. If I didn't, he would have found out eventually. Nevertheless, my choice had been made, and everything about my life was about to change significantly.

The enlistment ceremony was scheduled to be performed in the big city two months after I signed the papers. In the meantime, an envelope came in the mail, which surprised me because I seldom received mail. My heart skipped; I took a deep breath when I turned the envelope over. It was from a university in the northern part of the state that was prestigious for its music programs.

My heart started beating slightly faster as I carefully began opening the envelope. I pulled the letter out, unfolded it, and began to read. My body weakened, and I quickly sat on the couch. This letter informed me that I had received a full scholarship to study music at BG University. It was a benefit of winning the state music competition.

I could not believe what I had just read. Did they tell us the winner of the competition would get a scholarship? They may have, but I honestly didn't remember. If they did, how could I have forgotten something like that?

What am I going to do about the army? I wondered. *The papers have been signed. I can't get out after signing, can I?*

The letter was too late; it should have arrived sooner. Or did I let my impulsiveness get the best of me and make me join the army too abruptly? Thinking about the predicament further and weighing both options carefully, I decided not to try to get out of my enlistment. It would have been too difficult to do even if it could have been done.

Anyway, the army offered me the perfect opportunity to become a soldier like on television, travel to unique places like on television, and meet countless people worldwide like on television. Regardless of my musical ability, a gift I will always have, the army won out over attending a university in the same state, and it fit my objectives perfectly.

The Pledge

We woke to a warm morning with sunny skies when enlistment day arrived. Mom fixed an excellent breakfast because we knew it might be a while before our next meal.

After eating, we dressed, piled in the car, and headed to the big city for the swearing-in ceremony. As we approached the city, I became anxious.

What have I gotten myself into? I wondered.

My yearning to discover firsthand all that might be available to me could be accomplished only through a world-wide resource. The army offered such an opportunity. Along with faith that no conflicts would occur during my tour of duty and a strong belief in God's word promising protection, I did not have fear or apprehension. Being a little nervous about what lay ahead was a natural reaction to be expected. It was also exciting to me. These factors, in combination, justified my decision to leave and fulfill my desires.

More people than I had expected showed up for the ceremony; they kept coming through the doors and filling up the seats. After escorting my family to their section, I went to the desk to report in. The emcee began the ceremony, and my body shook nervously while I sat in my chair. When the emcee finished explaining the procedures, the time had come.

This is it! I thought.

He told us to stand, raise our right hand, and repeat after him. Our final words were "So help me, God!" and it was done. I had become a soldier.

Everyone in the massive room clapped and cheered, and my family glowed with pride. It was the proudest day of my life. My dad was particularly proud because he had also served in the army; I was following in his footsteps again. Other families in the room also showed joy and pride for their loved ones who took the pledge.

Next, we received orders revealing where to report for basic training and where our first duty station would be.

My respiration increased as I read the first page of the orders, as it told me my basic training would take place at Fort Gordon in Georgia. That was the same state my two Southern friends in the old neighborhood had come from. I was being sent down South for my training. Another television daydream was coming true. Now, not only would I see it with my own eyes, but I would live there too.

As I continued reading, the excitement of going south was dashed when I saw where my first duty assignment would be. They were sending me to Germany.

Germany, of all places.

Everybody knows it is usually cold there, and it's known for its brutal winters. I did not want to go to a place that had colder winters than where I lived. That crushed my expectations. I wanted to go to Panama. Some say a man is not supposed to cry, but I was a teenager. After reading that, knowing it couldn't be changed, I couldn't hold back the tears.

Due to the excitement, activities, and disappointing news about my duty station, I gave little thought to what basic training would be like. On television, they showed soldiers lined up in rows exercising, running in formation down a road, and training for physical combat. It was apparent there would be much physical conditioning and other activities that I didn't think would be too challenging for me. Still, there would be so much more to becoming a soldier, and I could hardly wait to begin.

3

JOURNEY OF LIFETIMES

Into the World

"The journey of a thousand miles begins with one step."—
Lao Tzu.

Before we left home, my parents prayed over me for my safe
travels and eventual safe return. As we pulled out of our
driveway and started up the street, I looked back, knowing
three years would go by before I would see my home again.
The mood was somber during the ride, and my parents
made light conversation. My emotions were a mix of
sadness and excitement; I spoke little during the trip.

Looking out the window at the scenery passing by, my
thoughts settled on my adoption. I wondered about my
name.

"Mom, why did you give me this name?" I asked.

"Because I like it," she answered with finality as if not
wanting the conversation to continue.

I paused and thought for a moment. Maybe she liked it because it was the name of a president, and they gave me my middle name to acknowledge my grandfather on my dad's side. They never told me if I had another name at birth, which would remain a mystery for years. Whatever their reasons for giving me that name, I thought it was unique, and my signature portrays its distinctiveness.

When we arrived at the bus terminal in the big city, the massive room echoed with the voices of travelers waiting to board their buses and others waiting for arrivals. We made our way to the check-in desk, and after the clerk gave me the ticket and showed us which gate my bus would leave from, my parents and I walked through the crowd to the location. Our timing was perfect; we didn't have to wait long. A line quickly formed at the gate after the loudspeaker announced my bus's departure.

Being emotional could not be helped; this separation would be a considerable time away from my family. Only once had I been separated from them for any length of time. That was when I accompanied my disabled cousin to a camp for children with disabilities. I was humbled that our parents trusted me enough to let me be there with him, but I was too young, and what was required of me, I could not do. The camp staff contacted my parents, and they came and picked us up before the course was complete. I still feel regret about it, even though I believe he forgave me in his way.

This separation would be longer and different in all aspects. It would also be challenging; only this time, there would be no chance of leaving before my tour of duty was complete.

The line moved slowly as the passengers began boarding. As I stepped onto the bus, I looked back at my family and waved goodbye, trying not to let them see me cry. I quickly dropped my head, turned, and walked down the aisle to find my seat. Fortunately, my seat was on the left side of the bus. When the bus backed out of its gate and began to pull out of the station, I saw my family through my window as they continued waving goodbye.

I couldn't begin to imagine their thoughts and feelings at that moment. My emotions were still mixed, but I became more excited as the bus pulled out onto the street and headed for the airport.

Everything imaginable about my future came to mind; my thoughts were unrestricted. My wish had come true, and my prayer had been answered. My journey into the world had begun.

ONE OF MY childhood dreams was to fly a plane—a fighter jet, to be exact. Watching their powerful take-off, graceful flight, and sometimes acrobatic maneuvers and smooth landing thrills me. While this would not be a fighter plane, nor would I be flying it, it would still be a plane. I experienced some apprehension because this would be my first time flying. Everyone, at one time or another, knew of airplanes falling out of the sky and people dying. That was my only concern, but I remembered my parents' prayers and my faith that God would keep me safe from harm, which calmed my nerves.

There must have been hundreds of people walking in all directions, the massive terminal echoing with all their voices. Waiting for my flight was almost unbearable; the anticipation burned inside me as I watched all the planes take off and land. The names of major cities across the country lit up the colossal flight display board, and the announcements came simultaneously. They finally announced my flight boarding an hour after my arrival.

That anxious feeling resurfaced as I gathered my luggage and headed to my gate. A lengthy line had formed at the security checkpoint, so getting on the plane would take some time. As I boarded the plane, I was amazed by its structure and interior design. Hundreds of seats on both sides and in the middle, in sets of three, ran along the plane's length, and the luggage compartments overhead matched the curvature of the aircraft. My seat was between two people, leaving me little room to relax.

After all the passengers put away their luggage and sat in their seats, the seat belt sign lit up, and the pilot made his announcement. My heartbeat increased as the plane jerked forward and began to move slowly down the runway. As the aircraft started to accelerate, few people spoke, and my prayers intensified as the engines grew louder, the plane moved faster, and the front end lifted off the ground.

It kept climbing higher and higher, higher and higher, thrusting my body into my seat. Then, the whine of the engines decreased as the plane finally leveled out. Still, my body didn't relax. I waited for the pilot to speak. When the pilot announced we had reached cruising altitude, I thought to myself, *That was intense.* Nevertheless, we were in the air, and I was on my way to basic training.

About two hours after our departure, we landed at the airport in Columbus, Georgia. Upon entering the terminal, military personnel directed me to the transport that would take me to the base.

Idle chatter could be heard during the ride about what to expect when we arrived, but my focus was elsewhere. The landscape we passed was breathtaking, just like on television. Only this time, I was there in real life. I could feel the warmth of the Southern sun on my skin, and I was breathing the Southern air.

When we pulled up to the gate, it was an impressive structure with guards on each side. The bus rolled slowly through the streets; most buildings were barracks where soldiers lived during their training and where I would now live during mine. We slowed and stopped at a building where several sergeants with distinctive hats awaited us.

When the bus came to a complete stop, our driver said, "This is your new home, gentlemen, for the next six weeks. When you step off the bus, do exactly as you're told, and you should be okay."

Developing Attributes

"Welcome to hell! You are now the property of the United States Army!" yelled one drill sergeant as we all began to file out of the bus. He screamed in our faces, telling us to hurry, grab our belongings from under the bus, and throw them on the ground. When I cleared the door, I quickly grabbed mine and threw them where he pointed.

Another drill sergeant got in my face and continued yelling, telling me to line up, stand at attention, and not move a muscle. I did exactly as he commanded; I stood there with him yelling in my face, and I did not flinch an inch.

The hectic encounter visibly shook some of the other recruits. When they didn't do as told, the drill sergeant made them drop to the ground and do push-ups; the count was always ten. Only half of us managed to avoid the penalty; the ones on the ground struggled to finish, and some had to do it twice. After that shocking experience, everyone finally stood at attention, and the drill sergeants ushered us into the mess hall for our briefing.

During the lecture, they explained what to expect during training and how to respond to the sergeants. Whether a drill sergeant told us to do something or asked a question, our reply must always be "Yes, Drill Sergeant" or "No, Drill Sergeant," appropriately. The instructor explained we would learn the traditions, tactics, and methods we needed to be successful in the army and beyond. During our basic combat training, we would become physically fit and learn marksmanship, first aid, military drills, and more.

When the briefing ended, they ordered us outside, and we stood in formation again. Two corporals came and handed each of us bedding for our bunks. We retrieved our belongings and returned to the formation to await our barracks assignments. Luckily, my assigned building was close to the mess hall where we stood, so I didn't have to walk far.

Everyone found a bunk where they wanted to sleep, put their belongings in the locker, and waited for dinnertime to arrive. That allowed us the opportunity to find out about each other. The members of our platoon represented almost every state in the Eastern region. A variety of ethnicities were represented as well. After we introduced ourselves, our conversations focused on what else the drill sergeants might have in store for us. Whatever it might be, nothing would come close to the unrelenting barrage we had encountered when we arrived.

Our training was rigorous. We would wake early, before sunrise, to begin our physical conditioning. After completing our exercise session, we would strike out on a demanding two-mile run. Sometimes, the sergeants made us run three or four miles with backpacks on our backs. Running those extra miles required significant effort, especially with the excess weight in the pack. The number of cigarettes I smoked reduced significantly.

OVER TIME, we all came to know each other more personally by working together as a squad, platoon, and company. Most established close friendships with those with similar backgrounds or perspectives on life, which made some comfortable enough to share any secrets they had. During our downtime, one afternoon, one of my new friends came to me and asked if I wanted to get high. Now, we were on a military base, in basic training, and closely monitored by our sergeants.

How did he get marijuana on the base? I wondered.

He told me how he did it, and I thought it was a clever plan because it had worked. I would never have taken the chance. I thought about it, but even my bold nature wasn't that daring, and I probably would have gotten caught.

We walked across the backyard to the woods, stood behind one of the trees, and started smoking. I don't know what type of weed it was, but it almost had the same effect on me as the acid I'd taken in high school.

Yes, I did acid in high school, but I did it only a few times because I wouldn't say I liked the trip, being outside my mind, so I stopped after the third time. The last time I had smoked marijuana was before leaving home for duty, which was probably why this high was so intense. Our walk back to the barracks seemed longer as we talked and laughed about everything. When we entered the barracks, one person asked questions; my friend let him join us from that moment on.

SOME OF US partied in the city when they gave us time off on the weekends. While there, a few of us paired off and separated to explore what else the city offered. Not all of us returned to the base after a night of partying; some rented motel rooms and stayed out the whole time. One friend and I shared a room one night; the attraction was attentive and mutual.

During our conversations, my friend revealed that we weren't the only ones sharing attractions. That's how he had found out about another person; they both shared their interest in each other. I was told to approach the person due to my fascination with them, but I declined; the interaction would have overwhelmed me. Plus, I don't get with someone after someone I know has been with them.

Most of us came to know about each other, keeping our preferences discreet. During one exercise called a bivouac— a simulation of battlefield strategies—they paired two of us up as partners. Our immediate orders were to set up our tents and dig a foxhole five feet deep. It took us until sunset to finish; by then, it was time to eat our military rations, which were ready-to-eat meals in cans or pouches made for an engaging culinary experience. Everybody had their favorite meals; my favorite was the green eggs and ham in the can, with salt and pepper for taste.

After our meal, we lay in our tent, getting to know each other better. The subject of needing a shave came up, and they asked me to feel their face. I slowly rubbed my hand over it, but I had to stop. It might have progressed if not for where we were; the chance of getting caught was too great. So, we settled into our sleeping bags, they in theirs and I in mine, and our attraction returned to subdued.

I knew of only those in my platoon, but by observation, there seemed to be more. However, it wasn't the time or place to show our attractions publicly or become expressively attached. We were not only to become soldiers but also men, which is what they expected of us. Most rose to the occasion and weathered everything the drill sergeants managed to throw at us; only a few buckled under the pressure.

At our graduation ceremony, they pinned our first stripe on us—another proud moment of my life. They took pictures and served dinner afterward to commemorate the occasion.

It was done; I made it through basic training without receiving any infractions, which was a miraculous achievement. I was physically fit. They taught me how to fire a rifle, how to fight in combat, and how to survive on the battlefield. For the latter, I could only pray and continue to have faith that I would never be exposed to such a horrific event.

Basic training was one of my life's most intense and challenging experiences; nevertheless, I faced what seemed insurmountable odds and became a qualified soldier. Advanced Individual Training (AIT) was where I would learn my job, Military Occupational Skill (MOS). When they offered us a choice of skills during the recruitment process, I chose a Signal Corps Combat Radio Operator (31C) designation because it appealed to me the most.

Skill-Based Instruction

Several shelves along two classroom walls held these big green radios with switches, buttons, and dials. Some were smaller, allowing soldiers to carry them on their backs. Several benches and wooden crates around the room held various parts and supplies. I remembered the radios from watching the television show *Combat!*, which was about an Army patrol unit that drove military jeeps with those radios on them through the desert to combat enemy forces. I loved that show, especially the jeeps speeding through the sand, jumping dunes, and spinning to a stop when they reached their destination.

As a child, I was naturally interested in radios, as evidenced by how I dismantled our old family radio to see inside. Radio communications were a significant part of my music entertainment experience, but this would be far different from civilian transmissions. During our training, we studied army radio call sign designations using the NATO Phonetic Military Alphabet, just like they did on the show *Combat!* It was so cool doing that.

We learned about radio mechanics, installation techniques, and electrical principles, though I can't say wiring was my favorite part. Through tests and exercises, I earned the Combat Radio Operator designation; another proud moment was when they pinned my second stripe on me at the end of the course. It was an educational and captivating experience in which I worked diligently to excel, ultimately graduating at the top of my class.

Preparing to deploy overseas was intense for me; I did not want to go to Germany! Nevertheless, like a good soldier, I swallowed my dissatisfaction and did what was required of me. As we traveled through the beautiful countryside on our way to the airport, a feeling of uncertainty and fear of the unknown suddenly throbbed in my chest. I didn't know why it hit me like that, but I encouraged myself to look at the positive aspects, which decreased the intensity of the doubt.

Transposed Expectations

Looking out the window, I was mesmerized by the big, fluffy clouds leisurely floating by; some caressed the plane's mighty wings as they thrust us through the sky. The view on this flight was spectacular and also intimidating. Trying to spot land was futile; the ocean-blue water below us stretched to the horizon and merged with Earth's blue atmosphere.

Flying over the Atlantic Ocean to Germany required a layover in Greenland, a continent close to the North Pole. Known for its frigid temperatures, it was freezing when we landed, but thankfully, we didn't have to stay long. That was, unfortunately, just a taste of what to expect during my tour in Germany. My dissatisfaction reemerged.

Frankfurt Airport, the largest in Germany and among the world's busiest, was uniquely structured. Its main twin runways seemed longer than those at other airports, at least by my observations. Four massive terminals extended from the center structure, with dozens of planes parked at the gates, forming intricate petal-like circles when seen from above. The architecture of the building was awe-inspiring, as was the number of people crowding the airport. All the concourses bustled with activity as hundreds of people walked in all directions to reach their destinations.

The weather was tolerable when we arrived, which slightly tempered my displeasure about being there. A five-ton army truck, our transportation to the base, awaited when we walked out the main door. With all military personnel accounted for, we climbed into the back of the truck and headed for base. Most minor roads were made of cobblestone, making for a bumpy ride at times; nevertheless, this was an opportunity to see the German countryside in real life, and the view was that of a living postcard.

Our base was inconspicuously situated within one of the smaller cities in southern Germany. All buildings and barracks on the small military installation dated back to at least World War II, and the preservation was remarkable.

When we arrived at my unit, we stopped at the battalion headquarters building, jumped off the truck with our belongings, and stood in formation to receive further instructions.

One of the sergeants stood in front and gave each of us our company assignment. They assigned me to the battalion headquarters and asked if I could drive a manual shift.

"Yes," I answered enthusiastically, even though the extent of my experience was in a stationary vehicle. I knew what it required from watching others drive. They then gave me my duty position: the battalion communications officer's jeep driver.

I could hardly believe my ears. I'm going to drive the battalion communications officer's jeep, I thought, my heart rapidly beating in my chest. I imagined myself driving a jeep, watching the television show *Combat!*, and playing in my dad's old car.

They also told me that my jeep was equipped with two radios that relayed transmissions from one location to another during field exercises. I thought that was so cool—not one radio but two. This was indeed a vital assignment that came about due to my class performance and my knowledge (somewhat) of how to drive a four-speed stick shift.

I would, without a doubt, rise to this occasion as well.

My company was designated battalion communications, and the basement of the mess hall served as our base of operations. That's where I got to know and began working with the others in my platoon.

One person looked familiar. As we spoke, and after a short brainstorming moment, we remembered where we had seen each other. We had attended the same training class together at Fort Gordon. Graduating ahead of me, they had deployed to Germany several weeks before my arrival. We had seen each other only in passing; nevertheless, the recognition was beneficial, and we became instant friends.

My new friend took to me early on and introduced me to the lay of the land in more than one way. Our battalion had five companies, each housed in three buildings near one of the installation gates. Through the gate across the street on the corner, there was a German pub they called a guesthouse. From rich, smooth wines and the wood barrel-flavored liquor to the darkest smoke-cured beer, their alcohol was far superior to anything I ever drank back in the States.

But on the far side of the base, just outside another gate, was another guesthouse we frequented more often. My new partner and I became regulars at the pub, even establishing a tab-to-pay later account. That courtesy was also extended to someone new to our company, joining the two of us who already shared the recognition. My attraction was immediate. We patronized these establishments so often that the owners and staff treated us like family. When we ran out of money, whatever we asked for, even food, they gladly provided because we honored our tab every time.

With unlimited access to their stock, we could drink to our heart's desire and get others tipsy as well. It seemed like the best way to bond with someone was over a few drinks. Many soldiers stationed there had a daily habit of drinking, and some even drank throughout the day; it was a common occurrence. Since we shared rooms, it was normal for several people on each floor to have liquor, beer, or wine in their possession.

We often started drinking in our rooms before hitting the town, but if our supplies were low, we'd swing by the guesthouse across the street. Our social activities revolved around drinking and partying, allowing us to loosen up and have a good time together. To aid in our relaxation, there were supplemental mood-altering substances that became known to me shortly after my arrival. One was caffeine powder, which some sniffed through a tube, producing a rush that lasted for hours. But it just wasn't my thing. The other, a condensed form of marijuana called hashish, was smoked in a pipe or on a fashioned pop can. With my partiality to marijuana, hash became my other drug of choice.

Between the two pubs, we had the power to shape situations and influence others to join in the fun. We often pursued new arrivals, and before long, certain individuals in our barracks were relaxing and enjoying themselves with us. It was an unspoken bond we all shared. Meanwhile, one person did not become relaxed but developed a disturbing interest in me. Sometimes in passing and often after formation, this sergeant would approach me, speak suggestively, and begin air-punching at me as if pretending to hit me.

One day, while I was walking toward my barracks after our last formation, they suddenly appeared beside me when I reached the door. When they started swinging at me this time, I threw up my hands to block their attack. Somehow, their head moved in front of my hand, and I punched them hard in the face.

Instinctively, my body turned instantly, and I ran at top speed to escape. Since they were shorter than me but endowed with muscles, I could not take the chance of them getting their hands on me. I had embarrassed them in front of the entire company, which, to their ego, was unacceptable. To get through the front yard, onto the street in front of the mess hall, up to and through the motor pool, back to the barracks, and up to my room took only minutes. I think I lost them in the motor pool. They never caught or confronted me that day, and strangely, they never approached me again after that incident.

A week later, Friend One and I decided to go to our favorite guesthouse on the other side of the base. Happy and talkative, we were in the best of moods when we walked in the door. We looked around and saw that the place wasn't packed yet. We spoke to our server, Rosie, who showed us to our seats and took our orders. After a short while, I excused myself to use the restroom. While doing my business, two guys entered and asked me if I knew a specific person. When I answered yes, one punched me in the head, then both began beating me all over my body. When I dropped to the floor, they started kicking me repeatedly.

My only escape was to crawl into a stall between the toilet and the wall so they couldn't get to me. When they decided to give up and leave, I stayed frozen in place from the shock of the event. My body throbbed with pain as I pulled myself off the floor and stumbled out of the stall.

Stopping momentarily to steady myself, I realized they had been sent by the person I had mistakenly hit in the face. It was that person they had asked about. He had put a hit out on me.

After managing to stand up straight, I rushed out of the restroom and stormed through the bar, motioning for my friend to follow.

After explaining what had happened, I asked Friend One if he had seen them when they came out. He said no, which I thought odd, but disbelief and anger might have manipulated my thoughts.

The next day, I told my first sergeant about the incident, and he called the sergeant into his office to get his side of the story. He lied, of course, and I was told to manage my activities better to avoid future troubles. So, because of someone's twisted fascination with me, I was humiliated by having to walk around with two black eyes for almost a month. All because of something they initiated. That didn't seem right, but I couldn't prove it, so there wasn't anything I could do except let it go.

Eventually, my curiosity wandered beyond our little neighborhood, and I began exploring the base more thoroughly. On one of my solo ventures, I walked to the commissary store to buy a few items and to the liquor store to replenish my stock. The long, enclosed hallway tunnel along the front of the commissary and liquor stores was often packed with people moving about shopping. As I walked through the tunnel and maneuvered through all those people, I noticed someone with butterscotch-cream skin standing at the far end. Instantly, everything began moving in slow motion, etching that moment in my memory forever.

What I saw overwhelmed my attraction; my heart started beating faster as I approached them. As I drew nearer, an excited sensation flowed through my body. I couldn't believe how fine they were and couldn't take my eyes off them. I wanted to talk to them, ask their name, and hear their voice. But uncertainty deterred me when I came within steps, and I spoke only by nodding as I walked by.

My trips to the commissary became more frequent, and an intense desire drove me to befriend this person at the next opportunity. Eventually, we saw each other again, and I managed to speak this time. We had interesting conversations about our units, the country, and other thought-provoking topics. After a while, we became comfortable enough with each other that I was invited to their room to relax for the night. After explaining to the duty guard that we were cousins and I had recently arrived, we were allowed to proceed. My "cousin" showed me to the room; my heart fluttered when we entered and fluttered faster when they closed the door.

They motioned me to the bunk on the bottom as my place to lie for the night, and at that moment, something about the situation didn't seem right. My attraction to this person was tremendously intense; I became anxious as I walked toward the bunk, wondering if I should leave or not. After lying on the bed momentarily, I looked up at them, at how appealing they were, and instantly, it was decided.

"I can't do this," I said. Then I got off the bunk, headed for the window, and climbed out.

As I returned to my unit, I felt disappointed, embarrassed, and like a failure. I can't imagine what that person thought of me or how it made them feel when I climbed out the window. After all that effort to become acquainted with this individual, at the moment of truth, I couldn't go through with it. What was so significant that it made me climb out a window to escape the situation I had begun?

The answer was that I knew the eventual result of the encounter.

I don't remember seeing that person again, but others from different units became acquaintances as time passed. We sometimes gathered at someone's barracks to drink and smoke before going out or to wind down from the day. During some of those gatherings, we learned of party spots in other cities. My partners and I decided we would visit every club mentioned. We made plans to first go to the Disco Tech in Nuremberg, the closest club to our city. High-speed commuter trains connecting all major cities were our mode of travel. Again, something I had seen on television and dreamed about doing was about to come true.

As we moved at speeds of over one hundred miles an hour, the ground, buildings, trees, farms, and small towns whizzed by as if we were in an aircraft flying at ground level. It was my first time on not only a train but a high-speed train, so it isn't easy to express the excitement I experienced during our trip.

Pulling into the station added a grand finale to the experience. The structure was intricately modern in its design. As I walked through the tunnel to the steps and up to the street, I felt like I was in a scene in a futuristic movie.

Mercedes-Benz had cornered the taxicab market in Germany; every taxicab on the road was a Benz. It would be my first time riding in a Mercedes. As expected, the ride was smooth and quiet. Everybody in Germany drove fast, like race car drivers, and the taxi drivers were no exception. Actually, they drove faster than most. Regardless of the intense ride, our driver got us safely to the club in no time.

The disco club was enormous. I couldn't believe my eyes. Bright lights lit up the building and the property surrounding it, and we could see flashing lights coming through the front glass door. When we entered the establishment, we walked straight to the bar, ordered drinks, and turned to look at all the beautiful people partying as if they had not a care in the world.

The club was packed, and everybody mingled without hesitation. Seeing the mixture of nationalities was like being in a candy store surrounded by every flavor of candy imaginable and unable to decide which one to taste. After dancing with my friends and visiting the bar a few times, we surveyed the scene to find someone else to dance with.

Unexpectedly (although, not really), my eye noticed butterscotch-cream skin standing beside one of the booths. As I began walking through the crowd, my stare did not waver. The closer I got to the person, the more I felt the attraction awakening, encouraging me to introduce myself and propose dancing.

My friends once told me that my tendency to be bold and direct was evident when someone looked attractive to me. Anyway, from the moment we stepped onto the dance floor, then through the night and into the morning, everything that happened that weekend was like a dream. That feeling lasted for weeks.

~

WE USUALLY TRAVELED BY TRAIN, but after I had been stationed there for a while, my first sergeant agreed to sell his car to me. I believe he decided on this because of my position and performance of duties. It was an honor to have been given this privilege. So, my very first car was a blue German-made Volkswagen Beetle a little larger than the riding lawnmower I drove as a child. Regardless of its size, I was proud to have it.

Someone called my friends and me The Three Musketeers because we were often together after duty. We decided to take a fourth musketeer along on this one trip, so Bug was full. We visited a club near a small mountain town several kilometers from our city. Somehow, they had carved into the side of a mountain to make the club, and it was the most unique construction I had ever seen.

When we entered the building, we immediately began drinking, socializing, and dancing the night away.

It was an exciting trip to the club because of the winding roads and spectacular views, and experiencing such a remarkable manufactured phenomenon was more than worth the drive. All of us enjoyed the mountainside spectacle, as was evident as we stumbled and laughed on our walk back to the car. As a result of consuming excessive alcohol, I went into a conscious blackout, remembering nothing about the return trip. It was a miracle that I drove those narrow, winding mountain roads to our base in that state of mind without having an accident and killing all of us.

Frankfurt was another of our favorite destinations, and Stuttgart was next on our list. We planned to leave for Stuttgart one Friday and return on Sunday to be back and ready for Monday's formation. On the day we planned to go, right before our formation, Friend One told us they had to perform a duty that weekend and couldn't go; we would have to go by ourselves. Friend Two and I had already packed and were eager to begin our trip. This was an unexpected development; it would be my first time partying in a new city without my number one. They understood our disappointment but assured us they were okay with the situation and sent us on our way.

IT WAS as if we were moving in slow motion; German automobiles raced by us on the busy expressways they call Autobahns. I wanted to go faster, ached to go faster, and tried, but my little Beetle Bug wasn't up to the task. We rode through beautiful valleys and over snow-covered hills as the autobahn mapped our way to Shangri-la. I mean Stuttgart. According to our sources, the club scene in Stuttgart was like attending Studio 54 in the States. You might see anyone who was someone, and whatever you desired would be available there. It promised to be an extraordinary experience.

For some reason, driving into this big, beautiful city thrilled me. The architecture was simply unique and exceptionally impressive. Hundreds of cars crowded the streets, some not even known back in the States. Every German we spoke to was friendly and welcoming; their disposition toward us was exceptionally notable. After asking several people, some of whom understood us more than others, we finally got directions to our destination. The club wasn't too far away.

I don't remember anything between when we found the club and when I woke up two days later in a hotel room with someone from the club. My heart started racing when I realized I'd woken up late. Friend Two was to meet me at the train station because we had separated on the first night of the weekend. Gathering myself quickly, I hurried out of the hotel room, through the lobby, and to my car. We had to leave at a specific time to be back and ready for Monday's morning formation. Thankfully, I made it to the station on time, but my friend was not there. I decided to wait and give them time, but I couldn't stay long.

After I had waited about ten minutes, it looked like they wouldn't show up, so I left without them. I figured they could always catch the train and get back in time. I found my way to the autobahn and proceeded on my way back to base. Cars whizzed by me effortlessly, and I noticed something intriguing. If a vehicle was traveling too slowly in the fast lane, the car behind it flashed its high-beam lights to signal the car ahead to pull over so it could pass. Of course, Bug and I pulled over and stayed in the slow lane as we rode toward the city's outskirts.

Suddenly, Bug's oil light came on, and she started sputtering and slowing down. It was quite a distance to the nearest exit, and though I tried to keep Bug going, she slowly rolled to the side of the autobahn and stopped. When I turned the key, trying to start Bug again, it only made a churning sound, and nothing else happened. It was like a scene from a thriller movie when a driver's car stops and they can't get it started again. My heart began to panic as cars zipped by at speeds bound only by their capabilities.

Sitting in my car, completely distraught, I didn't know what to do or where to seek help. Indeed, the experience was worrying; it was the first time I had ever been stranded. Being stranded on a high-speed superhighway made it even worse. I questioned my decision to leave without Friend Two. *Would this have happened,* I wondered. *Or would we both have been stranded together?* I could only hope that they had caught the train on time so they could make it back to our barracks for duty.

Finally, in the distance, the faint, distinct sound of a European police vehicle siren became louder as it approached my position. When the car stopped behind me, two German police officers exited the vehicle, and one walked up to me, speaking in broken English. He asked me about my difficulty. I told him I was a soldier returning to my base and explained that my car had run out of oil and stopped. The officer understood, motioned me to his car, and told me to get in. He called for a tow truck, which arrived quickly. They don't allow disabled automobiles to stay long on the autobahn's shoulder strip.

We pulled away from Bug, and I was chauffeured in a German police cruiser to a German police station where I would stay as a guest until they found someone to help me return to my base. I had not imagined something like this happening, nor had I wished to do this in any of my television daydreams. At least there were no restraints.

When we arrived, the police gave me blankets and toiletries, then put me in one of the cells as my waiting room. They even provided a cold-cut sandwich, chips, and a soda pop for a snack. I appreciated their hospitality; even so, being in that jail cell gave me an eerie feeling, even with the door open.

I heard several voices talking, some making phone calls and others discussing me in their offices. They put forth quite an effort, doing everything possible to help, which lasted most of the afternoon. Later that evening, they told me that someone from the military installation nearby would return their call in the morning. With that statement, any prospects of returning to my base in time for Monday's formation were permanently wiped from reality.

They woke me early in the morning to take the phone call from the military base. I explained everything, and they immediately sent someone to pick me up and take me to their location.

THE DRIVER INFORMED me that all their sedans had been assigned to other duties that day, and the next availability to take me to my base would be the next morning. When we arrived at the military installation where I would stay, I met with a first sergeant, who had words of concerning wisdom to share. Then she told me where I would stay for the night. It might have been a coincidence that the name of the barracks was the same as my last name. I still wonder about that. Aside from that curiosity, I was grateful to have a bunk to sleep on, a place to shower, and a full, warm meal. Even though I appreciated their generosity, it was a step up from a jail cell at a police station.

When they put me in a room with the only available bed, I met my new roommates, and the questions began. It was a strange and uncomfortable situation to be in; I did well to maintain my composure. Some thought I was new to their company, and when I told them part of the real story, they were stunned. One of my roommates took to me, which put me at ease, and we spent the rest of my time there together. That night, a sergeant told me when my transportation would depart to take me back to my base.

When we pulled away from my namesake barracks the next morning, the only thought that came to mind was, *What will happen to me when I get back?* I also thought about the people I had just met. What on Earth must they have thought about me?

When we arrived at my unit, my company was outside, just released from formation. So everybody saw me, even Friend Two, when I walked up. Nobody had to tell me where to go; I went straight to the first sergeant's office to await my fate.

After receiving a stern reprimand and being reminded of other previous infractions, I was subjected to disciplinary action. Naturally, I was taken off the promotion list, and it would be some time before I would become eligible again. They withheld money from my pay, and I was restricted to our unit for a month. Fortunately, I was shown mercy, and he didn't reduce my rank, which seldom happens with that disciplinary action. As for my first sergeant's car, when I told him what happened to Bug, his attitude toward me shifted noticeably for the rest of my time there.

As a result of several incidents that could have been avoided, my reputation as a model soldier was ruined. This one wouldn't have happened if I had checked my car beforehand to ensure she was travel-worthy, but Bug was my first car, and I hadn't been told to do that. Thank goodness I remained the comm officer's driver. As the driver, I was to ensure my jeep always remained operational. To do that, I would occasionally have to go to the motor pool maintenance bays if something needed attention. That's what made the Bug situation problematic.

At the far end of the mess hall, six maintenance bays stretched parallel to the length of the sizable vehicle enclosure they faced. They were noisy, dirty, greasy, and dusty; it was somewhere I did not visit often. To that point, an incident occurred with my jeep, one of the indiscretions considered in that disciplinary punishment. My spare tire had been flat for several weeks, and I hadn't fixed it before we had another flat while on field maneuvers.

The command staff, especially the comm officer, was incredibly angry with me. He had to find other transportation for the rest of our time there, and I could not perform my duties without my jeep, which put me in an unfortunate predicament. Our battalion's communications did not go as smoothly during our return to base. There was no radio relay vehicle to perform the process, so they improvised using two jeeps with one radio each.

Fortunately, I had made a respected acquaintance who worked in the motor pool—someone I had once approached. We established an understanding only to be friends, and their continued respect for me was reassuring. Since they were one of the better mechanics who worked in the motor pool, I explained how much I didn't like working there. They kindly offered to fix my jeep's tires and assist me whenever needed; they even talked me into working with them on my jeep a few times. Even with the fix, my command still held that lapse of responsibility against me. Nevertheless, the depth of gratitude owed to my mechanic friend during that time cannot be expressed in words.

AS A RADIO RELAY STATION, my jeep was crucial in guaranteeing uninterrupted radio transmissions between all vehicles in our convoy; that's why keeping my jeep and radios in superb condition was imperative. Our convoy, composed of various heavy military vehicles, stretched for miles and crawled at a snail's pace compared to the civilian automobiles that raced past us on the autobahn.

Grafenwöhr, pronounced Graffenveer, a region in Eastern Bavaria, Germany, is where our live fire field maneuvers occurred. A vast forest and snow-covered hills lay beyond the town, and our convoy had to travel around a mountain to get there. That's where my jeep comes in. The comm officer and I drove to the highest elevation ahead of the convoy, chose our position, and prepared to transmit. We worked in shifts, monitoring the radios. As the lead vehicles rounded the mountain, radio chatter increased and continued throughout the night.

The trailer I towed behind my jeep was where I slept when I was not on duty in the field. After all the vehicles had reached the forward position, my officer woke me up, and we descended the mountain to meet them. The roads were usually covered with snow, making them perfect for obstacle driving. As we zoomed through the forest and down the mountain, the four-wheel drive proved its worth by churning up snow and mud beneath all four tires, creating an unimaginable excitement within me. It was like how they drove their jeeps on the show *Combat!* I was having so much fun.

Our encampment was in a vastly unpopulated area, and on weekends, some of us were allowed to go into town to pick up supplies or have a drink. One morning, during my last field exercise with the battalion, I decided to go to town alone, and I followed the directions to the letter. After gathering a few items and a quick drink, I left the way I came. At least, I thought I did, but I must have made a wrong turn somewhere. Panic swelled in my chest because, as hard as I tried, I couldn't find my way back to the main road.

This training area was so vast that other military units from different bases in the country also trained there. I eventually stumbled upon one of them while trying to find my own. They escorted me to their encampment to see if they could pinpoint where my unit was, which took most of the day, but they were successful in the end. It was late evening when I reached my battalion, and my command staff was furious with me. This was another of the infractions expressed in the disciplinary punishment. Yet, even after all that, I was allowed to keep my private first class rank, which was amazing to me.

The consequences of my extracurricular activities extended beyond the infringements of my resulting disciplinary measures. As a result of engaging in hasty, carefree behavior, I often faced various health concerns. A medical professional cautioned me about the potential consequences, including the risk of infertility, if another health condition were to arise. While I wasn't actively contemplating parenthood at that moment, the warning served as a reminder to prioritize my well-being and better consider my choices in pursuing personal satisfaction.

MY TOUR in Germany did not happen as I had expected when I shed tears of displeasure about going. Aside from my unintentional transgressions, it was a party for three years of my time there. I learned to drink like the Germans, which I believe was how they tolerated the cold temperatures. It worked for me. I drank and partied with countless nationalities and ethnicities. Not often did I sense racial intolerance, bias, or tension—just people living, laughing, working together, and having fun.

However, my first three years left me feeling unaccomplished and like a failure as a soldier in some ways. My reputation could have been less revealing as well. I wasn't satisfied with leaving the military with such a questionable record, so after talking to the other Musketeers, we all chose to reenlist together and change our MOS from communications to administration. Performing field duty was no longer appealing to me; I hated being out in the field. After our leave of absence, our next duty assignment would be Fort Jackson, South Carolina, for the Administration School.

WE DECIDED to visit each other's city during our leave, and we picked mine first. Friend Two would leave a few weeks after us and go straight home to Detroit; Friend One and I would go there after visiting Friend One's family and friends in Philadelphia. While in my hometown, Friend One and I stayed with my parents, who extended every courtesy. They treated my friend like royalty, and that made me feel proud. We toured the city and visited some family and friends but didn't drink or get high out of respect for my parents.

On a whim, I thought about my old high school artist friend, so I decided we would pay a visit, and I would introduce the two of them. My old friend, Trey, standing at the top of the stairs and holding the door open, prevented us from entering and did not invite us in. The conversation was uncomfortable, and some pointed comments were made. It was an embarrassing exchange; it revealed how my old friend felt about me leaving without notification and bringing someone back to meet them. I'm quite sure by the look on their face and the verbal exchange that they came to the wrong conclusion about Friend One and me showing up together.

After that troubling encounter, it was time to leave my hometown for the next highly anticipated venture. Nothing could have prepared me for what I would experience in Philadelphia. I faintly remember words of a song describing a place as the land of milk and honey. Well, if I were to give a place that characterization, it would be Philadelphia. We engaged in casual drinking and smoking, and of course, we partied in one of the well-known clubs. Everyone I was introduced to treated me with much kindness and respect, and with one, my attraction was direct.

There were fascinating monuments, historical landmarks, and cultural events almost everywhere my friend took me. As I was driving through the city, the housing impressed me. On the outskirts, sizable homes with large lawns sat away from the road. Within the city limits, the apartments or condominiums were not built horizontally like in my city, but vertically in rows that were aptly called Row Houses. When my friend took me to visit somebody who lived in one, I was amazed by the beauty of the architecture and decor.

According to my happy-place meter, Philadelphia was among the most remarkable experiences I had ever had. I hoped that our visit to Detroit would register the same.

I was sure Friend Two had everything planned for our arrival. As expected, when all three of us came together, it was as if we were back in Germany again. We sat still only when we ate, changed clothes, or slept. There was always somewhere we had to be; Friend Two was extremely popular.

When the time had come for all of us to leave, I honestly didn't want to. If I had gone AWOL, that's where I would have stayed—there or in Philadelphia. When we arrived at the airport, it was buzzing with activity, with people checking in and others walking in all directions trying to catch their flights. Our check-in went smoothly, then we boarded our plane on time and were on our way. Going from the excitement of the big cities in the north to an army base in South Carolina, I expected it would be a starkly contrasting social encounter. Either way, I was eagerly anticipating the experience.

Practical Requalification

I was drawn to the impressive landscaping as we drove through the base entrance. Beautiful, precisely trimmed shrubbery lined the base of every building, and thick, healthy, freshly cut green grass layered the gently sloping hills. Weeping willow trees stood tall along all the smoothly paved streets. It was like riding into an artist's masterpiece. There seemed to be an atmosphere of serenity in the air and among the individuals there.

Upon completing our orientation, my friends and I were assigned to various companies, diminishing our chances of seeing each other often. Our instruction focused on managing military personnel records, composing letters, and finalizing orders and military honors. Given my profound interest in English, the nuances of the procedures seemed almost inherent to me. This new job would not only have me stationed at a desk in the warmth of an office but would also keep me from being out in the field, digging foxholes in the dirt.

The entire course progressed smoothly, concluding seemingly in the blink of an eye. Our ventures beyond the base were infrequent and primarily devoted to sightseeing or acquiring souvenirs from the local store. Nevertheless, as the course reached its end, the time arrived for us to discover our respective duty stations. Despite our requests for paired assignments within the same base and unit, the powers that be chose to send the three of us to separate locations across different states. Fort Bragg, North Carolina, emerged as my designated duty station. Regrettably, The Three Musketeers dissolved, and we were never to cross paths again.

Years after my separation from the military, Friend One somehow managed to find and reconnect with me, and to my surprise, wanted to visit me where I was at the time, so we met up for a happy reunion. However, there was a sedate undertone to our conversation and to their mannerisms. After the bewildering visit, several more years passed, and I decided to track down both of my old comrades at separate times. As I reached out to their families, my heartbeat slowed, and my breathing became more difficult as each family member informed me of their passing. Even now, my heart feels heavy at the thought of them succumbing to the illness when I have not.

I HAD HOPED the army would keep me in the South. It wasn't Panama, but it was close enough. I couldn't get enough of the weather. It was comfortable at night, warm in the mornings, and hot the rest of the day until evening. There were seldom any freezing days like the ones where I came from. Many people I came across in the South exhibited a similar warmth of personality and hospitality. Their welcoming spirits made anyone comfortable when invited into their homes. As a result, I developed a deep affinity for the South and the people I met while living there.

Expanding Horizons

Fort Bragg is the most extensive military base in the United States and is equivalent in size to a small city. It was renamed Fort Liberty on June 2, 2023, and is home to the Airborne Corps Special Operations Forces. It has all the amenities needed to cater to its sizeable population. The base is located northwest of a moderately sized city and adjacent to an air force base to the north. In addition, the air force base incorporates a smaller town, making the area an intriguing geographical grouping.

Upon my arrival, I was led to my assigned barracks and introduced to my roommates. We exchanged pleasantries, then they showed me to my bunk and helped me adjust to the daily routine. My roommates possessed lively, friendly, and inquisitive personalities, which I found reassuring. As time progressed, our shared interests helped establish a natural bond. Although the atmosphere in our room was pleasant, lively, and amiable, I felt uneasy walking through the hallways alone, being so new to the company.

One day, while I was walking down the hallway, the sound of pool balls caught my attention. Following the sound, I found the room. When I entered, everyone there looked at me as if I were an oddity, making me more uncomfortable than before. Not deterred, I thought this to be the perfect opportunity to play a game, meet the others, and give them a chance to meet me. As we played, they slowly became more friendly. In the end, after I had beaten two of them, we established mutual respect.

Not everyone in the barracks carried themselves amicably, as was apparent when I was walking to take an early shower one morning. As this person approached me, their gaze made me hesitant to speak, but I nodded in recognition of their presence. After I entered the shower room and had begun preparing to take my shower, I turned to see that same person standing at the door looking at me. Doing my best not to show how nervous they made me, I began a general conversation. My handling of the exchange must have worked because when our conversation ended, the person welcomed me genuinely and walked away.

Meanwhile, one roommate became more attentive toward me, and we started hanging together when not on duty; they even invited me to their home one weekend to meet their family. Only after I had known this person for some time and they had opened up to me and trusted me enough to meet their family did I allow the strength of my attraction to be known. I anticipated a mutual response, and the reciprocal encounter left me with a permanent mental image of the morning sun outside my window shining through the dewdrops on the leaves of the trees.

THE ARMY ASSIGNED me to the Personnel Records Processing Center in the US Army's First ROTC Region Headquarters. To my surprise, the facility was a charming single-story building situated relatively isolated from other structures on the base. It was surrounded by meticulously positioned and trimmed shrubbery and placed within a vast expanse of vibrant, well-maintained greenery, creating a picturesque landscape panorama.

Upon entering the building, I noticed the offices lined along the right side. As I continued walking, I saw on the left a large room that housed approximately twenty-five desks, where specialists diligently performed their duties.

This bustling hub of productivity dominated about two-thirds of the building.

Someone escorted me to my desk near one of the windows, which gave me an excellent view of everyone answering phone calls, typing on their typewriters, and shuffling papers back and forth. It felt like I was part of an old-school newsroom in a movie. I took immense pride in my work there, handling the cadets' paperwork, promoting them to lieutenant once they met the requirements, and processing their orders to transfer them from training to their active duty stations. It made me feel like a valuable member of the army recruitment process.

After the two-year delay due to that disciplinary punishment for misconduct as a private, I finally received my promotion to specialist fourth class (E-4). Despite the setback, I had excelled as a soldier and in my job since then. Shortly after I was promoted, they assigned me to a different personnel unit on base. I was pleasantly surprised when my coworkers threw me a going-away party with cupcakes, fruit punch, and even a pen set as a parting gift. Although I would miss everyone, I looked forward to meeting and working with new people.

As with every military unit, our company began each day with physical conditioning. After showering and dressing, we ate breakfast and headed off to work. When I arrived at my new duty position, the person who would train me came to my desk with an armful of records. After a brief training period, I was on my own, and over time, I became one of my section's most skilled records processors.

While working there, I formed friendships with the

others in my office, and my supervisor was especially helpful whenever an issue arose. I also had the chance to meet people from other organizations on the base, some of whom became good friends. One evening, during a dinner conversation, someone mentioned the theater on the base, which reminded me of my acting experiences during high school. I jumped at the opportunity to audition when they mentioned an upcoming play.

Meeting more people from the base and nearby cities who participated in all aspects of the production was an enriching experience. But after a particular hour, most nightly activities in the two towns ceased, leaving us only two choices for socializing after rehearsal and the production. Most of the action happened at the enlisted members' clubs at Fort Bragg or the air force base. They could be just as intriguing as a civilian club; sometimes, the approach was even more direct.

When we grew weary of the base clubs, we traveled to other destinations to party and enjoy ourselves. Atlanta, Georgia, was everything I was told it would be and more than I could have expected. Like Philadelphia, the city was host to countless references to and recognitions of African American heritage, most of which I did not know existed. Filled with an atmosphere of pleasantry and goodwill, it drew me in with the charm of it all. If one night can be defined as the inspiration for a phrase, never had a fruit tasted so sweet.

～

SOME OF THE new friends I made lived off base, and when I explained my urge for change, they suggested that I move off base as well. It was more affordable to live in a trailer than an apartment, and trailer parks are common in the South. An opportunity suddenly presented itself, and I hurried to sign the lease. This was my first time living independently, so I made sure not to move far. I packed my belongings, moved in, and began living the life of a bachelor. By then, I was in full swing with the social scene and started meeting more people. One caught the attention of my attraction, and my pursuit automatically kicked in.

At first, everything happened as anticipated. We exchanged phone numbers and began talking often until we eventually came to the first visit. I will not lie—I was mesmerized by what I saw. Nothing could draw my attention away. The attraction became overwhelming. They moved in after only a few visits, and I thought we were the perfect pair. We lived off base, so we could share the bills, buy food together, and still have money for our drinks and weed. Most importantly, we would have someone to come home to—a companion and friend.

The breakdown in trust began with them coming in late and some nights not coming in at all. When I questioned them, an argument ensued and lasted until they left again. I couldn't understand what had happened to our arrangement, but something had changed. Eventually, they moved out entirely, leaving me with the bills and rent. This had to happen right when the electricity bill was due, and I didn't have money to pay it. So, the electric company cut off my electricity on the shutoff date, and I was left alone in the dark and cold.

Lying on the couch with my head under my thickest blankets to keep warm, I struggled with the reality of what had happened. Suddenly, someone knocked at the door. It was my section sergeant looking for me. I had missed work on that Monday. My trailer was freezing cold, and when I opened the door, a rush of cold air hit my sergeant in the face. The reprimand was stern. He demanded that I put my affairs in order and return to work immediately.

I should have realized that if the person so strongly appealed to my attraction, they would be that appealing to someone else. When someone finds themselves attracted to someone new, they must decide whether to honor their current relationship or not. This person did not, and I suffered rejection, humiliation, and abandonment because my attraction demanded immediate satisfaction.

SOME JOB TASKS become tedious over time, and a person might look to do something out of the ordinary, even spontaneous. At this point, my record processing had become second nature, even dull. I longed to do something different, something additional, something new.

One day, during our morning briefing, the section sergeant announced that the 82nd Airborne Corps would be holding airborne training for anyone who wanted to participate in the course. I really didn't bother to think it through, so it didn't take long for me to decide. It was, in effect, the answer to my predicament, and I did not hesitate to sign up.

It began with a rigorous physical conditioning program, not unlike basic training; only this course had additional elements incorporated. It had been raining before our first day, so the training field was laden with soft, muddy soil and random muddy puddles. We couldn't help splashing mud all over ourselves as we ran around the course, climbing over and beneath wooden barriers; they even erected large poles with thick ropes that we slid down to practice our parachute landings. It was even more fun than basic training.

With each day that passed, the instructors added to our routine as we advanced to each subsequent stage until the moment to perform had arrived. We piled into the back of a truck and headed to the air force base, where our C-130 aircraft awaited. As the truck rolled onto the runway and stopped, it reminded me of the military shows I had watched on television that showed troops boarding the backs of those huge planes. In real life, they were gigantic.

I could feel the power of its engines as we walked by, and they idled with a moderate hum. The exhaust warmed the air behind them, creating a visual mirage. In rows of two, we walked up the massive rear ramp of the plane and sat in the seats on either side. They told us to strap in, and the engines began to wind up as the aircraft started to taxi to the runway. By now, the excitement of doing something so drastic to liven up my life started to seem extremely risky. But I had passed all the training and classes, and I couldn't back out even if I had wanted to, so I had to see it through.

As we cruised hundreds of miles above the Earth's surface, every part of the massive aircraft seemed to vibrate as the engines powered us through the sky. Our instructor restated the procedures they had outlined in class. When our plane approached the drop zone (DZ), where we were to land after jumping out of the plane, the ready light came on, and we stood up to connect our static line to the rope overhead.

When the yellow light appeared, the instructor yelled, "Stand up, hook up! Stand in the door!"

We all stood and hooked our static lines to the rope

above, then the person closest to the door walked to the door and stood. At the same time, the door opened, and the force of the wind whipped through the plane, making us tighten our grip on our static lines.

When the green light appeared, the instructor yelled, "Go!" With a tap on the shoulder, the first person jumped from the door. Like beads on a broken necklace, those in line before me filed out behind him. When I stepped up to the door, half of them had jumped out. My heart was racing, and with doors open on both sides, the wind seemed to want to pull me out. I only hesitated momentarily. Then I jumped up and out as instructed. The instant I jumped from the plane, the wind snatched me away.

The static line connected to our main parachutes, and after we reached a certain distance from the plane, it would open the chute and detach.

As soon as I leaped out and up, I shut my eyes. It wasn't until I felt the sudden jerk of the parachute opening that I finally opened them, and what a sight it was to behold! I was left speechless as I gazed upon the spectacular view of the Earth's horizon and curvature, all without the aid of a plane.

As I slowly descended through the sky, a serene silence caressed me and the gentle breeze whispered in my ears, a sensation unlike any I had felt before. As the ground approached rapidly, I followed our training, placing my feet and knees together and preparing for the imminent landing. As I neared the ground, a sudden wave of fear gripped me, causing me to wet myself. I thought I would have done that when I jumped out the door.

Despite this, the experience of parachuting became a cherished pursuit, offering an unparalleled, tranquil experience as I floated through the Earth's calming atmosphere and gazed at the horizon. Many coworkers couldn't imagine themselves making such a choice. Even though it seemed a drastic undertaking, I found fulfillment in the freedom, peace, and pride it brought. Each day, I returned to my duties, and I eagerly anticipated the next opportunity to leap out of the plane and into the sky again.

During this three-year enlistment, I consciously tried to improve my overall conduct. My drinking and smoking had decreased dramatically compared to my time in Germany. As a result, I was hoping to secure another promotion without any delays. Despite being busy processing a stack of personnel records at my desk one day, I gave my section sergeant my full attention when he walked up to me, handed me a set of orders, and told me they were reassigning me to a newly reactivated unit for deployment overseas.

Never could I have imagined, nor did I consider, that just doing my job would gain me recognition from higher commands, especially after the brief time I had been working there. I was engrossed in my responsibilities, carrying myself professionally when on duty, and keeping my personal preferences discreet. Yet I was unaware they had been watching me so closely. To be selectively chosen and assigned to this unit was the most significant moment of my military career.

Essential Obligations

How many times in one's life can they say that their dreams became a reality? Okinawa, Japan, the island north of the mainland, was magnificently scenic yet surprisingly crowded. What seemed like thousands of people occupied the relatively small island, with houses built close together and apartments stacked on each other or above restaurants and family stores. Hundreds of cars, primarily compact, crowded the narrow city streets and highways. I mostly enjoyed the seventy-degree temperatures; that was my atmospheric comfort zone.

Being assigned to and working in the headquarters of the First Battalion, First Special Forces Group, Airborne, was more than a dream come true. It was an honor and a privilege only a select few would obtain. I was now a part of the elite US Army's version of the Navy SEALs—only we came by air, and they, by sea.

My first sergeant took me under his wing and taught me how to process the operational paperwork for the soldiers assigned there. As before, I caught on quickly, settled into my duty position efficiently, and, with unyielding dedication, became proficient at performing my duties.

More troops were scheduled to arrive since the unit had recently been reactivated, so the office was usually busy with activity. I was the third records specialist to arrive, and out of the five companies in our battalion, they assigned two companies to me. The others maintained the rest. We processed all personnel action orders, special operations orders, and more, all of which, in the end, had to be approved by higher command.

The first sergeant's charge was overseeing all clerks and administrative activities in the headquarters, coordinating arrangements with the personnel records office when promotions and awards were to occur, and reporting to the command sergeant major and full-bird colonel battalion commander for final approval. Since I worked in the headquarters building, my duties sometimes required that I submit documentation to both. So, I saw and spoke with each of them often.

Not long after my deployment and arrival on the island,

I was promoted from a specialist to a sergeant (three stripes) and moved to the front desk. Everyone entering the headquarters building had to stop at my desk before proceeding to the person they came to speak with. My notoriety within the battalion skyrocketed, and I became a familiar face to everyone. The workload was heavy, but the more intense it became, the more skilled I became at keeping everything in order and knowing about all administrative actions happening in the office.

SOMETIMES, when I stayed in the office after an intense day and everyone had left, I finished the recordkeeping and prepared documents for the coming day. With the tranquil atmosphere around me, it was easier to concentrate on the job at hand. When I finished working, I left the office. But before going to my barracks, I might walk over to the hill on the side of the building. Night would have fallen several hours before, and the sky would be clear and full of stars. I would lie back on the hill and look up at the stars to let my mind unwind.

One night, while looking up at the vast expanse of stars above, my eye caught something moving among them. My glasses were on, and from what I saw, it looked like a star. Only this star was traveling in a straight line across the sky. I watched it pass by several other stars, and then it suddenly stopped. I continued watching, and it began moving again. That's when I decided it was time to go in. By then, I considered the phenomenon an extraterrestrial event; stars don't move in the sky like that. I promised myself not to mention the encounter to anyone because I was afraid of what they would have thought of me if I had.

Our installation was situated along the coast of the East China Sea. Our barracks and the headquarters building lined the shore. On occasion, I would walk down to the rocky beach to be alone with my thoughts. Few people went there, so I mostly had the whole beach to myself. As I gazed upon the expansive ocean, contemplating the significance of this once-in-a-lifetime opportunity, I would think about how I was on the opposite side of the planet from my home. Being there was, indeed, another response to my request to travel around the world. Those moments in my life were the most tranquil I had ever experienced.

It was customary in the service to hear stories about other countries—in this case, those in East Asia. Some older soldiers in our unit told of their experiences as we discussed what these countries offered in terms of getaway destinations, tourist attractions, exotic food, beverages, produce, and commodities. My deployments with our unit took me to Thailand, the Philippines, and South Korea, allowing me to explore and experience their people and cultures in person. Visiting these countries was like stepping onto a movie screen and coming out into the scene you had been watching in the movie.

Let's start with South Korea. I can't remember the purpose of our operation, but we stayed there for only about a week, maybe two. Part of being familiarized with the area included a tour of the Demilitarized Zone (border) between North and South Korea. The perimeter consisted of a fortified brick wall with machine gun posts at measured distances. None of the North Korean soldiers seemed friendly. Each of them had a military assault weapon in their hands or strapped across their back, and the expressions on their faces showed their contempt for our presence.

The country's atmospheric aroma reflected certain types of cuisines consumed, which I found disturbing. Kimchi is a Korean gourmet dish made of cabbage fermented in a dirt pit. The dish was typically served for dinner and had a pungent smell. We stayed at a military installation in South Korea, and the personnel urged us to experience Korean cuisine. Of course, we did. Unfortunately, nobody told me that kimchi is a spicy-hot dish; my mouth was not pleased. Despite the friendly and welcoming nature of the South Korean people, I have no plans to visit again due to tensions at their northern border.

WHEN I WAS in high school, everybody knew about marijuana from Thailand and the Philippines. Sometimes, we were told that what we were buying had come from either country. It did look different from the usual leafy-green marijuana we were used to. They also had other names for it in each country: Thai stick in Thailand and Gunja in the Philippines. I distinctly remember smoking Thai stick in high school, and it was good. While in the Philippines and Thailand, it would have been remiss of me not to compare the locally sourced weed to what I had smoked before.

As I walked through the streets, I spoke to random Filipinos, hoping someone would understand me. I finally found someone who responded to my request.

"Do you want gunja?" he asked.

"Yes," I said, nodding.

Then he led me over to one of the buildings that looked

like somebody should tear it down and told me to wait by the doorway until he returned. I will admit that my nerves were unsteady as I waited. I wasn't supposed to be by myself; it was evening and getting darker, and everyone passing by looked at me as if they knew why I was there. And they were right.

When the young gentleman returned, he handed me this big bag of marijuana and said, "Is this what you want?"

Again, I nodded, even more enthusiastically because I couldn't believe the size of the package. He had given me two times what I would have been given in the States for the same amount of money. My next thought was, *How on earth am I going to keep this amount of weed concealed as I travel back and when I get to our base?* While walking back to our encampment, my mind raced with thoughts of how to hide the weed. Then I remembered basic training.

When I reached camp, I went straight to my tent, found something in my belongings to hold that amount of marijuana, packed it in as tight as possible, and waited until the exercise ended. Getting through the security checkpoint would be the ultimate test to see if the concealment really worked.

Success: nothing showed on the screen when my luggage passed by, and the canines didn't pick up a scent. Wasting no time, I tried out the gunja when we returned to our base in Okinawa. As expected, it lived up to its reputation.

In Okinawa, marijuana was scarce. When available, they sold it in matchboxes, which cost twenty dollars apiece. Since the amount I had obtained was so plentiful, I decided to keep part of it for myself and a select few to smoke. I sold the rest to make money on the side. Eventually, I sold enough and made enough money to purchase a red Nissan 280Z from someone who was soon leaving the island.

~

When our unit held training exercises with the armed forces of other countries, they sent advance parties to get everything ready. I felt privileged to be included in the small contingent going to Thailand, and that's when I was introduced to the Thai people and their culture. My Thailand experience differed significantly from the Philippines expedition; I did not feel uncomfortable among the people there at all. In fact, I loved everything about Thailand, especially the people. Their rhythmic speech was pleasing to my ears, and the color of their skin enticed me.

When we arrived in Bangkok, Thailand, and reached the hotel, the lobby was bustling with activity. While one of the sergeants went to the clerk's window to check us in, we waited in the bar area and had a few drinks. While we were there, a couple of young Thai ladies began flirting with us. Only another sergeant and I were of the same ethnicity in our small group.

Because of that, I felt trapped in engaging in pleasantries with the women, not wanting to draw attention to my true desires. One of the stories I'd heard was about Thailand's streetwalker commodity—how beautiful and sensual the women were. It would have been ill-advised for me to return from Thailand and not be able to talk about my experience of that commodity.

So, after I received the key to my room and the conversation came to the price to be paid, the young lady who had latched onto me led me to the elevator doors. When we reached my room, we entered, and she immediately began to disrobe. Following her lead, I did the same, and we started to engage in the expression.

I'd had more than my fair share of drinks while waiting and was noticeably drunk; it was the only way I could have participated in the activity. However, I was unsuccessful in obtaining satisfaction for either of us. I was just too drunk, not into it, or both. Even though it was my first time with a female, I wouldn't say I liked the experience in any way.

The next morning, when we all gathered in the lobby to start our day, the sergeant of my ethnicity asked me how my encounter with the young woman had been. I think he knew of my preference, and the question was a test to see if I had gone through with the expression. I was honest and told him it didn't go as expected. It didn't help that the young lady was standing beside me when he asked the question, and she clarified my answer. She told him that I couldn't perform and that the experience for her was disappointing.

I couldn't have agreed with her more.

The following day, our lieutenant allowed us to go sightseeing but warned us not to go out alone. Of course, I ignored the warning and walked through the city streets by myself. I saw shrines and small temples where the Thai people gathered to pray, and they all had lifelike gold statues of Buddha. It was the first time I had seen gold and that much gold in one place—and outside in public. Crime was obviously not an issue like it was back in the States.

At last, I came across a street filled with social establishments, but none caught my interest until I reached the last one. Inside, a lively crowd of young Thai individuals caught my attention, and my attraction began to awaken. I sat at the bar, sipping drinks and admiring the beautiful people dancing. Finally, I called the bartender over and asked, "Who's available? And how much for one night?"

Upon entering the room, I was shocked by the overwhelming decor. The walls, carpet, and heart-shaped bed were all red. The language difference didn't matter; we knew why we were there and wasted no time sharing the expression between ourselves. I had never been with two people before. It was an experience I will never forget, and I'll leave it at that.

I returned to the hotel early the following morning, and everyone was still in bed, so no one saw me come in. I had succeeded in my covert mission to satisfy my yearning and express my attraction to not one but two of those beautiful people without anyone finding out.

After another encounter, which occurred in a hotel room in the city, my covert rendezvous was a success. Rickshaw drivers were abundant, offering an alternative mode of transportation to automobile taxis. A rickshaw is a Thai-powered bicycle-seat coach, and I decided to hire one on that day. During the ride, I became increasingly attracted to the figure in front of me. Eventually, I proposed an arrangement, which they accepted; we then obtained a room, and that's enough about that.

OUR ADVANCE PARTY was scheduled to return to Okinawa in two days, leaving little time to find some Thai stick to take back. But as it turned out, it was relatively easy. After I had asked three people, the fourth knew where to get some, so I followed him to the spot. When our transaction concluded, I returned to my room and pulled out the sizable amount of Thai stick I had bought. I split it into three parts, covered each with Saran Wrap, put each portion in its own cold cream jar, covered them with cream, and screwed the tops back on. The test would be getting through the airport security checkpoint equipped with an X-ray machine again without being discovered.

It had worked when I returned from the Philippines, but I had packed the items deep in my duffle bag, making them more difficult to detect. An anxious feeling made my heart beat faster because, this time, the probability of getting caught was higher. I packed my bags with the items deep inside, just like before, but the bags were smaller this time. The amount I bought could have been deemed possession with intent to distribute and the unlawful transport of a controlled substance across borders. If caught and arrested, I would face several years in one of their prisons, regardless of my military status.

As my bags slowly entered the machine, my eyes stayed trained on the officer monitoring the screen to see how closely he was paying attention to the contents going by. From where I stood, I saw my bags on the screen as they entered the machine. But the guard suddenly looked away to speak with someone. When he turned back to the screen, my bags had gone through without a warning or scrutiny. You cannot imagine the amount of relief that coursed through my body at that moment.

DURING OUR FULL battalion deployment to Thailand for military exercises with the Thai army, some troops asked me about the party spots. They described what they wanted, so I took four of them there. After visiting the bars and getting drunk, we entered the building with a flashing red light. We saw a large glass wall with young, provocatively dressed ladies seated on velvet cushions with numbers hanging from their necks. I couldn't leave the four of them alone, so I decided to pick a number and play the game. As expected, I didn't enjoy it. Later, when everyone gathered outside, we continued partying through the night.

After establishing our base of operations in the Thai Army encampment, we worked closely with our counterparts during the training process. The Thai soldiers' barracks were small one- or two-person manufactured straw huts constructed in rows of two that ran the length of the camp. One of my counterparts offered to show me his. Of course, not long after we sat down, he pulled out a Thai stick joint, and we started smoking. It seemed exceptionally potent, and it had a surprising effect on me.

We understood each other well enough to joke and laugh about everything, and then it happened. The individual asked the question; they sensed or saw it in me. I acknowledged their interest, and we expressed our attraction to each other. My head was floating as I walked back to the operations tent. I couldn't do any work, and I knew my condition showed in my demeanor, so I went straight to the makeshift barracks to sober up.

Being around and working closely with the Thai soldiers was a test of my attraction's restraint. One seriously weakened my resolve with their bowlegs and smooth, tanned dark-almond skin. It was challenging to focus on my task whenever they came near me. My attraction to this person was intense, but I could not reveal my desire. It was challenging to do, but I managed to maintain my composure, and we became comrades since we worked alongside each other in the operation tent with the command staff.

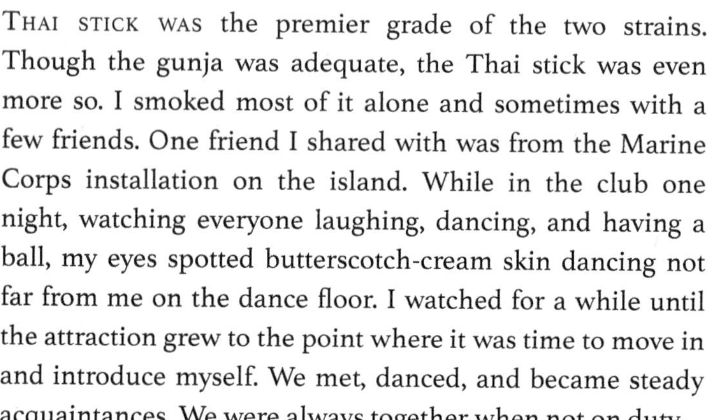

THAI STICK WAS the premier grade of the two strains. Though the gunja was adequate, the Thai stick was even more so. I smoked most of it alone and sometimes with a few friends. One friend I shared with was from the Marine Corps installation on the island. While in the club one night, watching everyone laughing, dancing, and having a ball, my eyes spotted butterscotch-cream skin dancing not far from me on the dance floor. I watched for a while until the attraction grew to the point where it was time to move in and introduce myself. We met, danced, and became steady acquaintances. We were always together when not on duty.

Within almost a year of being together, we moved into an apartment across from my base. But after being around each other constantly, our coupling began to fray. I devised an idea that I thought would liven up our relationship, so I proposed we be open to experiencing other attractions. There was one stipulation to the agreement: neither of us was to engage with one particular person who had shown interest in both of us at a party we had attended in someone's barracks one night.

We both agreed, but I was the one who kept my promise. My housemate did exactly the opposite of what was asked. It is impossible to put into words the feeling that gripped my chest the moment they told me they had been with the person. I was crushed. Technically, my suggestion had set the stage for the engagement. It was, in a way, a test to see how dedicated that person would be regardless of my request. They failed.

After that happened, I couldn't help but wonder how my friend from high school had felt when I joined the army and came back home with someone else by my side. Perhaps this experience was karma for what I did back then—leaving my friend in high school without notice. Now, being in this position, I knew they must have despised me then.

Apart from that disappointment, my life on the island was more gratifying than I could have imagined it would be. I was driving a sports car and selling and smoking marijuana every day, all day long. Everybody in the unit knew I smoked. I partied every weekend and sometimes during the week, jumped out of planes and helicopters, visited other Far East countries, gazed up at the stars at night, became one with the universe, and was the head administrative clerk in a Special Forces headquarters.

I couldn't have dreamed of a sweeter life.

4

DARKNESS FRACTURES LIGHT

Living In Uncertainty

It was a beautiful morning, as usual, and we all were mingling, laughing, and talking while finding our positions in the morning formation. Most activities for the day were routine; no special operations had been scheduled to take place, but the final announcement shook my being to the core.

The year was 1986, and all overseas military personnel had been ordered to take a test to see if they had been exposed to the HIV virus. It had become an epidemic that was ravaging the male same-gender-preference population, killing hundreds. If anyone tested positive, they would be returned to the States for medical care.

Immediately, I knew I had been compromised. Could it have been through same-gender transfer or by opposite-gender interaction? Upon reflection, I admit that I had initiated and consensually participated in numerous same-gender encounters. Yet I couldn't help but think about how many partners those young women had been with before me. They could have been infected by any of their previous customers, which in turn could have infected me. Everything considered, in either instance, I knew that the damage had been done.

Several sergeants informed me that my test had returned a positive result. They came knocking on my door at two thirty in the morning, ordering me to wake up. They told me to pack two bags and that they would send the remaining items to me after I arrived at my new unit.

"Your HIV test was positive, and we're transferring you back to the States" were the most alarming words ever spoken to me.

After I hastily packed my essentials and some clothing, they rushed me down the stairs, out of the building, and through a fog-laden night to the waiting ambulance. They hurried through the streets to the hospital on the air base and put me in an isolation ward. I was the only patient in the ward, and they made me wait for hours. Finally, several people came to me. One handed me a set of orders assigning me to Fort Polk, Louisiana. At that moment, my anger erupted, and I demanded to know what had happened to the standing orders transferring me to Fort Hood, where my cousin was assigned.

They gave some excuse, justifying the cutting of the new orders. I do not remember anything from that moment—not exiting the hospital, not riding to the plane, not flying back to the States over all that water, and not arriving at the airport. I can't recall any of it. I can remember, however, walking up the sidewalk to my newly assigned unit and handing my orders to a sergeant who happened to be standing outside.

The whole encounter was like being in a science fiction movie in which the people are transported into an alternate reality. I couldn't believe this was happening to me. Then I began questioning why the unit command had handled my case as they did. *Did others test positive?* I wondered. *Did they suffer the same humiliation as me?*

Maybe they did it because they knew of my extracurricular activities.

I'm almost sure everyone knew I was getting high every day. In fact, someone came to me and told me someone had asked them if I was still smoking that marijuana. It didn't matter. The damage had been done. However, I did write a letter to the commander and sternly expressed my displeasure with his handling of my situation. I hope it wasn't ignored.

BE THAT AS IT WAS, I showed up at this new unit unannounced, which raised many questions. Of course, I had to explain to my new unit's command what happened and why I was there. Then, others in the company began asking questions as well. Most questions came from the two other individuals housed in the old World War II barracks they put me in. The building was not equipped with air conditioning in the middle of August, and it was sweltering hot there. The little fan I bought at the commissary did little in the way of providing comfort, so my transfer was not off to a good start.

The phobia and fear associated with that disease had gripped the world, and those who didn't fit into that gender-preference community shunned those who did. Wisdom dictated that I not share my diagnosis with anyone outside the command staff, who, I might add, wasted little time setting up appointments for me to visit the nearby veterans' hospital.

Several people questioned me about my trips to the hospital, and over time, some of them started putting two and two together. Finding lies to satisfy their curiosities was challenging, but keeping track of what I had told to whom became impossible.

Those standing orders to Fort Hood were my reenlistment orders. I had served for nine years, and it was time to reenlist. When they called me to discuss the ceremony, I told them that if I reenlisted, I wanted to go to Fort Hood, like I was supposed to. They told me no and said I should have known it was impossible.

The staff sergeant said, "If you reenlist, you must stay at Fort Polk for the next three years."

With that statement, I decided to sever my ties with the US Army. I couldn't stay there any longer; the accusations, speculations, and rumors had become overwhelming. There was no way I could stay in that unit or on that base. I had to leave.

Going back home was not an option. I would not subject myself to the questions and rumors that would arise upon my sudden arrival there. Additionally, news reports about people with HIV said it mutated into a fatal strain called AIDS. After the transformation, most afflicted suffered debilitating diseases and died. It was a rapidly spreading virus, increasing the death rate each day.

What would my parents think about me coming home to die from a deadly virus? I pondered earnestly.

～

AFTER FIVE MONTHS of working through the requirements and studying the Non-Commissioned Officers' Development Manual, I had been placed on the promotion list to become a staff sergeant (E-6). This virus diagnosis ended all of that. It halted my entire military career, effectively derailing my life course. It was all over now. Done. Knowing the deadliness of the virus, I could only surmise that I might also die soon.

Until that time arrived, my priority was to find somewhere to live—or, more specifically, find someone to live with. Being stationed in Louisiana for about eighteen months allowed me to find party spots and interact with people. Considering these were people of my same gender persuasion, there was little to no phobia or fear. But there was a caution. Nevertheless, I was able to make friends shortly after arriving.

One friend, also in the military, lived off base with their partner in the nearby city of Anniston, Alabama, and they invited me to move in with them until I could get on my feet. I was not accustomed to being sheltered by people, and certainly not by people I barely knew. Despite that, their hospitality saved me from the embarrassment of going home. This friend's character did not indicate ill will; they seemed genuinely kind and caring. But they did like to enjoy themselves at times. During one of those get-togethers, aside from everybody drinking and smoking marijuana, someone brought something else to the party.

They kept their business private by locking themselves in the bedroom, but their secret eventually made its way beyond the bedroom door. Someone handed me a joint, told me it was laced with a substance I hadn't heard of, and asked if I wanted to try it. Both high and drunk and still in a state of virtual depression and denial about my diagnosis, I was primed to try this new drug.

The taste was unique, and it produced a tingling sensation in my brain that then coursed throughout my entire body. It was like the rush of the long-forgotten acid I had tried in high school or the crank I had tried in Germany. Only this rush induced a rapid blood flow to specific parts of the body.

From that time on, smoking my marijuana without this additive made for a bland high, so when I sought to buy one product, I bought both together. At first, my friend purchased the items for me but soon showed me where to go so I could get my own if they were unavailable. We left the apartment building one warm, starry night and walked two blocks up from the main street. Then we turned onto a side street, walked a little farther, and turned onto another street that was darkened by tall trees and broken streetlights.

Obscured figures lingered around the entrance of the one-block-long dead-end street in front of us. Two vacant houses almost hidden from view by the trees' shadowy overhang on the left side of the road seemed ominous at first sight, and the abandoned warehouse building to the right held the same posture. Beyond the barrier at the end of the street was a large grassy field with the ruins of another old building's brick foundation to the left. We found the person selling the products that night. We bought what looked like little white rocks, then returned to the apartment and smoked.

That was the usual routine during the weeks of my stay, and since there was no job to occupy my time, I was often left to go purchase on my own. There wasn't much activity at the spot during the day, so evening and night were the right times to score.

One weekend, after my friend arrived home from work, we began smoking, drinking, and enjoying each other's company. My attraction to this person had started when we met, but I had managed to subdue my desire out of respect for their relationship.

During our conversation, they expressed fondness toward me and eventually brought up attraction, but we also talked about their partner. I shouldn't have. I knew better, but the attraction was strong, and the door had been opened to participate in the expression. After that, being around and living with them became uncomfortable for me. I faced the other person daily, acting like nothing had happened, and my friend's performance was better than mine.

ONE EVENING, I decided to venture out alone, not wanting to be around my apartment mates so they could spend quality time together. I chose to go to the spot and hang out for a while. When I arrived at the block, someone approached me and asked what I wanted. I told them, and we began a conversation as we walked toward the barrier at the end of the street. We found someone, and the transaction took place. To my surprise, the person I was with asked me to continue walking with them. We began talking as we walked along the front of the ruins, and on the way back, we walked through the inside.

"This is where people come to smoke alone or with someone else," they said, pointing at two people sitting in the corner of what had formerly been a room. The first thing that shocked me was the apparatus used to smoke the rock. It looked like what was used in Germany to smoke the hashish. What they did to each other while smoking publicly was another shock; I would never have been that bold.

Not ready to return to my friend's apartment, I proposed smoking a joint with the individual, and we walked into the darkness of one house, sat on the porch, rolled up, and smoked. As we smoked and conversed, random people came by cars or walked from the adjoining streets to buy drugs. Some chose to stay, picked inconspicuous dark corners, and stood under tree shadows between the houses in an attempt to conceal their activities.

As I began walking to the apartment, I noticed how they constantly flicked their lighters without considering how bright they were in the darkness. Flicking lighters while doing drugs and other things in the dark put all of us at substantial risk of getting raided, and I couldn't afford that. It made me realize I could not continue this behavior. Something had to change. The only way to break the cycle and stop feeling guilty when around my apartment mates was to leave and move somewhere far away. Just not back home. Not yet.

WHEN MY SEPARATION from the army was imminent, I purchased a brand-new white Chevrolet Cavalier four-door sedan—my first brand-new car. Since the US Army was my employer and I was a first-time buyer, the conditions were favorable for the loan approval. I didn't tell them I was getting out. My experience with cars is extensive; I've forgotten most and will not attempt to recount them all, but I have owned many.

During my assignment at the base and while staying with my friend, I had the opportunity to meet people from all over the region. People from small towns and large metropolitan centers came out to party every weekend as the sun set. During one of our party outings, we visited Houston, Texas, to attend a special event.

The city's vast size was remarkable. Filled with intricately designed shiny towers and skyscrapers, it was a fantastic sight indeed. The streets bustled with people walking in both directions and crossing at every street corner, heading toward their intended destinations.

We eventually made our way to one of the city's most notable clubs, where we danced and partied the night away. As the evening ended, a new friend we had met in the club invited us to an afterparty.

We followed them to the location and heard the music as we neared the complex. A few people entering one of the apartments confirmed we were in the right place. The small residence was comfortably crowded, with just enough space in the living room for a few couples who wanted to dance. Four people were in a fascinating card game at the dining room table, and others lingered around in the kitchen, waiting for their drinks.

Being the last person through the door, I was left to ensure it closed. When I did, I glanced to the chair that the door had hidden, and that's when I saw butterscotch-cream skin sitting there. We looked into each other's eyes at the same time; our gaze was intense. The attraction was instant and powerful; everyone else in the room faded into multicolored figures framed around our stare. We continued glancing and staring at each other throughout the card game, and when the card game finished and that person stood, I couldn't believe my eyes.

There have been times when I have become physically weak when I've met someone exceptionally attractive to me, and this was such an occasion. What I saw was worthy of pursuit. They also gave all the signs of interest, and when we introduced ourselves and shook hands, the connection sparked an instantaneous tingling sensation from my hand up through my arm. We immediately exchanged numbers and then returned to the party and our friends.

When I returned to Anniston, I stayed connected, calling them often but not so much as to keep it fresh. During some of our conversations, they told me about their employment, where they worked, and what they did. When I shared about myself, I was honest about most aspects; I eventually spoke about my need to relocate, and they understood. They revealed that they lived in a house alone, so it wouldn't be a problem to let me stay if I wanted to move in. Plus, Houston had plentiful job opportunities, so the chance of finding employment was good.

I considered my present situation. I was living with a couple. I helped one cheat on the other, and I was spending time on street corners waiting to buy drugs and smoking drugs outside with other drug addicts in the dark of night. It was time to change the scenario before something unfortunate happened to me. So I called my new friend in Texas, and they agreed to let me stay with them until ...

The invitation was left open like that because we both shared a strong attraction to each other as interested parties, and indications were that we would become more than friends.

My apartment mates expressed concern about my sudden departure, but I began preparing days in advance. I revealed my plans to move only after my friend in Houston confirmed the relocation request. My possessions fit into my little Chevy Cavalier—the back seat, passenger seat, and trunk were all full. We said our goodbyes, and I drove away from the apartment building and headed for the interstate. My friend and I never saw or spoke to each other after that, and I figured that was best, considering the circumstances.

Getting to Houston would take approximately ten hours, but I loved driving, so that was fine. I was excited to move to the fourth-biggest city in the United States to live and hopefully have a stable and productive life with a prospective partner. Plus, being with someone so attractive and profound would be worth all the effort. The drive would also give me the opportunity for self-reflection.

I wondered, *How long will I live before succumbing to this deadly virus?*

Their Ways

Elliot told me the type of car they drove, and I was to look for it upon my arrival at the prearranged location. When I pulled into the parking lot and looked, I saw them. I motioned that I had arrived and followed them back to their house. Then they helped me settle in.

The home was the perfect size for a single family or couple. The style of the house, located on the edge of the city's metropolitan area, had to date back decades. They told me it was a historic landmark left to them by a relative.

Introductions to their friends happened quickly; I was the talk of their little circle. Most of their friends were the same gender as me, except for their female best friend, who was kind and welcoming.

It wasn't difficult fitting in; we all liked to party, but none used the other drug, which was a good thing. Everyone accepted me without hesitation because they knew my friend so well. They enjoyed many social and material advantages: they were popular among their associates, owned their own house, maintained substantial employment, drove a high-end automobile, and now had a reliable partner. Everybody seemed happy for them.

After settling in, I took it upon myself to do the cooking and cleaning to show my appreciation. Every day, I made sure dinner was ready and the house was clean when Elliot returned from work. Even though I was a stranger, this person allowed me into their life when my life was at a critical moment. I felt like I owed them at least that much.

We went to dinner one evening so they could show their appreciation and welcome me to the city. What set this dinner apart from your typical dining experience was that the location—the Hyatt Regency Spindletop, Houston's famous restaurant in the in the sky—offered a stunning view. I was astonished; from our table, the city lights stretched until the darkness eventually quenched their glow. Bringing me to such a luxurious place to dine in a distinguished manner made me feel welcome, worthy, and well-kept.

~

AFTER A BRIEF PERIOD OF SEARCHING, I was able to secure a job. I started working in clerical positions, moved on to data processing, and then soon applied to the post office. As a veteran, I was given priority over other applicants, which almost always ensured employment. Though I had never considered becoming a mail carrier, it was a job I was willing to do. I was pleasantly surprised by how much I enjoyed working as a mail carrier.

It turned out to be a delightful experience that exceeded

my expectations—traversing the picturesque neighborhoods, strolling across well-manicured lawns, and delivering mail to charming houses. It felt like I had stepped into a role on a television soap opera and was portraying the quintessential mail carrier. The nostalgia of my days as a paper carrier also surfaced. But, in that case, we threw papers in yards and occasionally on porches while pedaling our bikes past the houses.

Acquainting myself with the mail route was a breeze, and over time, I had the pleasure of meeting a few customers during the early morning hours. It was, without a doubt, the ideal job for me. I enjoyed working outdoors in the warmth of Houston's temperatures while performing my duties. This job was the perfect supplement to contribute to our income. Joy, happiness, contentment, parties, and passionate expressions had come into my life as well.

Everything seemed perfect over the next few months. Maybe it was too good to be true. Keeping things organized and clean had gradually become a challenge. Increasingly, clothing items lay all over the bed and in every room in the house, and the kitchen suffered dirty glasses, plates, and pans until I cleaned them up. The workshop area was in total disarray as well. It hadn't been like that when I had arrived. The change in Elliot's behavior concerned me.

Meanwhile, we were still attending parties, getting drunk and high, laughing, dancing, and having a ball. We always attended parties and went out to the clubs together. But on one occasion, I found their conduct on the dance floor to be insultingly expressive. When the coast was clear, I worked my way to the individual my partner had danced so suggestively with and asked their name.

With a stunningly perfect physique, radiant, smooth, dark-chocolate skin, and a head full of loose jet-black curls, it was clear why my partner had danced upon them as they did. I introduced myself, they said, "I'm Billy," and we began a short conversation. We exchanged phone numbers that night, and I assured them that I would call. Then we shook hands and returned to our tables.

EVEN THOUGH WE had little in common, some of my partner's friends had become mine over time, and we started hanging out when possible. One evening, one of my new friends thought enough of me to share an observation. It was about my significant other, and the news was not good. After being alerted of an indiscretion, I chose to keep the information to myself; it could have been the reason for the behavior change. Plus, I didn't want to confront them with a rumor and start a controversy about an unproven accusation.

One day, my significant other told me to expect a guest, so I straightened the house, anticipating their arrival. At the same time, they busied themselves preparing their workshop and barbershop, leaving me to open the door.

When the door opened, I had to catch myself so I would not react. This person, whom I had never seen before, was even more appealing than who I was with. Both seemed uncomfortable as they proceeded with their business. It was interesting that each time I walked by, that person looked at me as if I were coming in their direction, and I thought that odd.

Something else that caught my attention was how they spoke to each other in hushed tones, barely noticeable a room away. My feelings then led me to believe they were more than casual friends.

That was our relationship's first big red flag, but I maintained my position and did as a devoted partner would do. Some days following were tension-filled, and others were calm and settled. One day, I was blindsided by my partner's plans to attend Mardi Gras in New Orleans without me. The rest wasn't difficult to figure out.

While this happened, the post office assigned me a different route with a different supervisor, and my first impression did not go well. I was furious that they had changed my route, and after I expressed my displeasure, the supervisor had it out for me. After about a week of being on the new route, which I hated, I quit.

"You quit the post office?" some people asked. "Why?" they would ask in disbelief. Everyone agreed that my decision was drastic, but to me, what they did was unreasonable, unnecessary, and drastic. I am a veteran, so finding a different job was not a major worry for me. Or at least that's what I hoped.

MY MENTAL HEALTH did become a concern during the first week of my partner's absence. I wondered what they were doing and who they might be doing it with. *What must Mardi Gras be like in person?* I wondered. *Will my friend dance in the parade down their main street, wearing one of those hats like on television?* I imagined wild parties happening everywhere all day and night, any of which they might attend with their attractive haircut friend.

The whole time they were away, I didn't even receive a phone call to let me know they were okay. But I received a message at the start of the second week of their stay. The female best friend called on the house phone and wanted to speak to me. What was said destroyed the rest of my heart. My significant other had decided to stay in New Orleans for an additional week. Immediately, I knew why. And that was the end. It was over.

I needed to leave Houston before my partner returned. I tracked down and contacted an old childhood friend, Rob, the stomach-puncher, who now lived in California. After speaking with Rob, who understood and was sympathetic to my situation, we made plans for my arrival and stay. My friend told me about their job as a private security guard for a company specializing in hiring veterans. They believed I had a good chance of getting a position there as well.

I REMEMBER SAYING I liked driving; however, driving across the United States was not what I meant at the time. Due to the urgency of my situation and not wanting to see my ex when they returned home, I packed up my little Cavalier and headed to California without delay. Using a paper map, I plotted my twenty-two-hour journey through most of Texas, past New Mexico and Arizona, and finally through Southern California to LA.

Having music in my car is essential whenever I drive; it makes any voyage tolerable, no matter how long. There was no doubt I would be listening to a lot of music on this trip. One thing that made this trip different, though, was driving through the flat lands of New Mexico and Arizona. Looking out my window, I saw fields of grass and wheat stretching as far as the eye could see, and the roads, all smoothly paved, extended for miles without coming to a hill. It was the most comfortable drive I had ever taken. My new car rolled along effortlessly with no hint of stress or malfunction. The most impressive moment of my multistate drive was when I drove up and through the Rocky Mountains on the last leg of my trip to LA.

After I reached the summit of the lower mountains, my windshield became a modern picture frame for the perfect, true-life view of the LA city lights and the ocean shore beyond. I could not believe my eyes. The moon cast its light on the ocean waves below as the immense, sprawling metropolis lights shone like a beacon in the darkness of night. I'd never seen this scene in any of the movies I'd watched. It was incredible. The sensation of a new adventure coursed through my body as I drove down from the mountains into the city lights. I made it to LA and would soon be living among movie and television stars, as well as famous musicians like the one who married my cousin.

Incidental Reality

Located in a suburb on the city's outskirts, my friend's house had a large living room at the entrance, a dining room straight ahead, and a moderately sized kitchen to the right. Down the hallway were two bedrooms and a bathroom, but I would sleep in the living room during my stay.

Even with rest stops, driving that distance had taken its toll on me. So, shortly after I walked through the door, they handed me the bedding for the pull-out couch. I made it up, lay down, and didn't wake up until the following day.

The faint aroma of breakfast woke me from my slumber; having someone cook for me was a welcome change, a gratitude I will always cherish. My hosts worked during the day, and that left me time to relax and recover from the long drive and my previous circumstances. My heart was still aching from the betrayal.

Around the third or fourth day, lying around watching television became annoying because something always reminded me of my recent past. It was time to get busy, find something to occupy my time and mind, and push the depression away.

One evening, we all gathered in the living room to discuss my potential employment with my friend's employer. During the conversation, it was revealed that the security officer's job was with a well-known national discount drugstore chain. Rob described the position, and it struck me as both complex and fascinating. Background checks were required, but that wouldn't be a problem for me, having recently separated from the service and not having had any adverse legal history. My friend spoke to the supervisor and returned with a date for my interview.

While waiting to hear the results of the interview—which, by my estimate, went well—my friend took me to all the notable attractions in LA. I even saw the Hollywood Walk of Fame with my own eyes. Just think_I was that close to Hollywood stardom, and yes, I did look around to see if I could spot one.

The city of Los Angeles—with its delightful, pleasantly mild weather—enriched the overall beauty and lives of the people I met who lived there. Many friendly people welcomed me readily, and we had enjoyable conversations as cordial people do. One such conversation was with my new supervisor because I got the job! All the preparation I had done for the interview paid off. I started my orientation immediately, and they let me try by myself the same day.

The best thing about the job was that we did not wear uniforms; we wore everyday clothes to blend in with other shoppers. Inconspicuously observing people while shopping initially seemed like an intrusion of privacy. Consequently, I was informed that when in the store, privacy does not extend to the products until they are purchased.

As with any other job, except after the post office switched my route, I applied myself and soon became particularly good at spotting even the expert shoplifters. My schedule ensured that I would be at random stores on certain days; even the store management did not know when I would be there. After greeting them to let them know I had arrived, I would begin browsing the store like other customers.

Sometimes, I saw shoplifters stick objects in their pants pockets, inside their coats, in handbags, and in anything imaginable. The list is endless. Then I would stand in line behind them and watch to see if they paid for the item when they rang out. Confronting them outside after they left the store could sometimes get physical. Usually, the police were never far away when needed.

Some perpetrators I collared were young women stealing something they needed, and some young men stole just because they wanted to. It was sometimes difficult to determine which motives factored into the actions to be taken against them. If they told a compelling story, they might be let go with a warning. Others did not tell such a story and sometimes displayed belligerent behavior; the police took those away. On one occasion, my convictions were tested when I caught a college student stealing.

This wasn't an average person like most who came into the store to steal. This individual was endowed with the physique of a football player. They were slightly taller than me, so when I looked up at them, the unassuming guilt on their face made me emotionally sympathetic to their predicament. Back in my office, we engaged in a personable conversation about their educational goals and prospects beyond. My attraction to this person also factored into my final decision. But most importantly, I didn't want to be the person who stained their higher education pursuits. After sharing words of wisdom, encouragement, and a warning for the future, I sent them on their way.

A MONTH AFTER BEING EMPLOYED, I began looking for permanent lodgings. Fortunately, finding an apartment wasn't difficult; the vast metropolitan area and surrounding suburbs were teeming with many to choose from. One caught my eye; it was affordable and located in Riverside, an hour from LA. Getting to work would require extra travel time to whatever my assigned store would be. That would allow me to become familiar with more of the area. The renovated two-story hotel offered furnished studio apartments, and mine was on the second floor, near the end of the building as you entered the parking lot.

Hopefully, it would be a while before I would have to pack my car with all my belongings, move in, and settle into new surroundings again. Some things, small but sentimental, went missing with each relocation. Even so, I'd emptied my car and had all my possessions put away in my new apartment before sunset. While resting on my couch, I enjoyed listening to the calming and quiet evenings—even the sounds of the crickets in the grass surrounding the complex.

My life had taken a significant turn for the better. Since I was in such a good place, I sought out my cousin—the one married to the famous singer—and to my astonishment, we connected. We set up a date for my visit. I was looking forward to seeing her, but I was looking forward to meeting my famous cousin by marriage even more. I thought it would be cool to sing a song together, play around in a recording studio, and drop some tracks. This could be my big break. I knew that making that appointment was essential and that my life could be changed forever.

As the days passed, loneliness began to creep into my mind, and it didn't help that I still held ill will toward my Houston partner. Curious about Elliot's situation and eager for an update, I called our mutual friend, and she was very willing to give me an update. She said Elliot called her right away when they returned home. Their voice filled with sadness, Elliot told her my belongings were no longer there; I had left.

I didn't believe the emotional part, so I devised a plan to retaliate during my preoccupation. What if I called Billy the dance partner? I wondered. After all, I know they'd exchanged numbers with Elliot and had spoken since that night. They might have even been with each other since then. I just wanted to see how they were doing. As we talked, the conversation was routine until it turned to distress. They shared some of the difficulties they faced, and that's when I offered them a solution.

"Move to California and stay with me," I said. "I'll pay for your transportation and help you find a job when you get here."

They were very receptive to my offer and wasted no time accepting my invitation.

My plan worked. I'd pulled one of my ex-partner's interests from Texas to California to live with me. I was hoping they'd told my ex, and I wished I could have seen their face when they heard it.

Another benefit of moving my new friend to California was companionship. There would be someone there with me, waiting when I returned home from work. And I would have someone to share and express my emotions with. This person was extremely attractive but insecure, and I made it my mission to encourage them to accept their blessing.

The bus terminal was bustling with people, and their voices echoed throughout the openness of the building. Navigating through the multiple terminals with buses arriving and departing was a challenge. Eventually, I located the gate where my new companion's bus would park and waited patiently for their arrival. Once Billy stepped off the bus and gathered their belongings, we hugged and headed toward my car for the ride home.

When we arrived at my apartment, we got them settled in, and the following days and weeks felt like a new life. It was like I had been transported out of the uncertainty and into a productive existence with my new partner by my side.

Unfortunately, our joyous coupling lasted only weeks, until my partner suddenly began showing signs of a scalp infection. We both became frantic. Not knowing what to do, I thought of when my mother tended to my wounds and provided other first-aid treatments. I began caring for them without delay. It took a little over a week, but we managed to mend the sores and prevent the infection from spreading to the rest of the scalp.

After one month into our promising relationship and three months of working at my job, I was given the unsettling news that layoffs were imminent due to budget constraints, with the most recently hired being let go first. Once again, I found myself at the mercy of an employer's decision, leaving me with no alternative. In the short time I had been working, I'd developed connections with fellow security personnel and store employees, and I'd made new friends. My life finally was gaining momentum when it came to a screeching end.

One morning two months after losing my job, following my usual morning routine, I walked to the living room window and opening the shades to welcome the morning sun. As I glanced down to where my car should have been, I saw it wasn't there. Instantly, shock overtook me. Then I realized that my car had been repossessed due to my falling behind on payments. I used one month's payment to bring Billy; I didn't have the next month's payment due to the layoff. Consequently, I found myself stranded and unable to assist myself, let alone provide for my friend.

Facing that realization, we sat down to have a serious conversation about our next steps. We decided that my companion would head back to their home in Texas, and their generous aunt offered to cover the expenses for their journey. Unfortunately, I had no option but to leave California and return to my hometown. It was disappointing not to fulfill my desire to meet my cousin and her famous husband—a crucial opportunity lost due to circumstances beyond my control. Also disheartening was the lost opportunity to establish a lasting relationship.

Summoning up all my courage, I reached out to my sister and shared my current predicament with her. To my relief, she was very understanding and, without hesitation, offered to help me by purchasing a bus ticket to ensure my return home. No matter what my circumstances were, my sister always responded to my pleas, for which I am eternally grateful. Although the journey was long and some of the rest stops were unpleasant, it gave me ample time to ponder and meditate on everything.

One of the main questions I asked myself was, Did my act of revenge bring about the troubles of illness, a lost job and car, and the failure to make it to my cousin's place to meet her star husband? I recall the Bible verse Romans 12:19: "Dearly beloved, avenge not yourselves, but rather give place unto wrath: for it is written, Vengeance is mine; I will repay, sayeth the Lord."

I did not heed that warning, and to my detriment, I suffered the fate of disobedience; worse yet, I involved someone else's life in my iniquity. For that, I was being sent home to start over from nothing, reassess my priorities, heal, and devise a viable plan to survive again.

Strategic Retreat

You couldn't have found a person so thankful to reach the end of a bus ride or, more directly, many bus rides across several states. The trip was arduous, and I was so relieved when we pulled into my hometown's bus terminal that I said, "Thank God," aloud.

My parents, exceptionally joyful about my return, met me there. They took me back to the house, asking ordinary questions along the way but nothing direct or specific. However, when they asked for more detailed information, I avoided sharing that until later.

When we pulled up to our little house on the hill, I walked in and headed down the hallway to the bedrooms. I threw all my clothes on the floor, flopped down on the bed, and fell asleep until dinner. It felt so good to be home. Most everything in the house had stayed the same. Mom had bought new lamps for the living room, changed the window coverings, and replaced the coffee and dining room table settings, but those were the only changes.

Dad had covered the pool with the pool cover; it was fall, and swimming season had ended. The leaves on the trees along the back edge of our property had begun turning colors and falling to the ground. Now that I had come home, guess whose job it would be to rake and dispose of all those leaves.

Later that night, when we sat down for dinner, I divulged everything to them. I told them about my diagnosis and carefully selected details about my activities and movements after leaving the army.

My dad started his comment with, "Well." He continued by reassuring me that no matter my transgressions and ill-advised choices, God still loved me and that I must believe and have faith that God would continue to walk with me, help me back on my feet, and protect me from evil-doers. Mom and Dad always turned to God in times of trouble and did not hesitate to lift me in prayer.

That discussion went better than expected. I did not suffer the same fate as others who revealed their preference to relatives and were shunned for who they were. My parents had always known, though they never spoke of it openly. They chose to put it in God's hands, and their attitudes, treatment, and love for me did not waver at all.

After sufficient time had passed, allowing me to recover from that long ride and plan my next move, I started looking for a job. Since my previous employer was a national drugstore chain, I contacted them for a potential job opportunity. An interview was scheduled, and thanks to my experience with the corporation, they offered me the job on the spot. I started working at the beginning of the following week. As the new security guard in town, I had the advantage of being an unfamiliar face, so I easily mixed in with the other customers. I quickly resumed my duties, even catching seasoned shoplifters who thought they could get away with it.

When I received my third paycheck, I went looking for a car. I found one but needed a cosigner for the loan. Mom graciously agreed to do so. Being without transportation for three months, even a day, was excruciating for me. Nevertheless, I was mobile now and could arrive at any of the store's locations within minutes of leaving home.

Upon returning home, I was relieved that things turned out better than I had anticipated. My parents responded to my diagnosis and explanation of my movements with the utmost grace and support. I was healthy and did not show any signs of sickness. Catching a cold was a rare occurrence. Any apprehension that existed before was now removed; my secret was safe with only my parents and me.

As a result of what happened in the army and the months that followed when my life fell apart, being back with my family was a healing experience. Although it was great seeing my parents again and staying with them, it was time for me to find somewhere to live. Sometimes, during conversations, they threw little hints and made certain statements to that effect. I understood they had become accustomed to living without children, and since my situation had improved, it was time to give them their space back.

There was an apartment complex, located on one of the city's main roads, that was inconspicuously hidden by the surrounding tree shadows. You would drive right past it if you didn't know where and when to look. My apartment was at the end on the first floor of the building on the left side of the parking lot between the two-story buildings. Most tenants stayed to themselves, as I did, for a while. By this time, I was ready to start smoking weed again. By observing people around me, I found someone to ask.

This person visited other people's apartments periodically, staying only moments at a time, leaving again, or staying longer in others. It was familiar behavior to me. So the next time they came to my building and walked past my door, I stopped them and introduced myself. While speaking, something else familiar became apparent; my attraction took notice. At the time, after watching their comings and goings, it would have been inappropriate to pursue the interest; the priority was buying some weed to smoke, and my attraction returned to subdued.

The days and weeks that followed went smoothly. My job, transportation, and health were all in decent shape, and being in a new environment felt comfortable. From time to time, my contact would visit my apartment, and we'd have a smoke before they moved on to their next client. During one of these visits, we discussed their other customers, and I revealed that I was attracted to them by including myself in the comparisons. My attraction awakened again. Their response took me completely by surprise: a passionate embrace rather than dismissive words.

After our exchange, I was uncomfortable continuing to live there. Their visits to certain apartments made me feel envious even though I didn't know this person well enough to have this feeling. My attraction would not dissipate while I continued to deal with and see them, so before any more feelings became stronger or interactions took place, I decided the time had come to find somewhere else to stay. I felt an intense urgency to leave promptly.

I FOUND my new place much quicker than I'd found my previous apartment. I found a house for rent this time, and it was pretty close to my parents' place. This would be my second rental house. The first one was during my time at Fort Bragg.

It was easy to make myself at home in my new place. My parents gave me a thoughtful housewarming gift, and I rented furniture and purchased a television and stereo to make my living space comfortable. The house had a base-ment, a roomy backyard, and a garage accessible from the street. On the other side, two properties away, was an older brick building that used to be a school but now served as a community organization's workplace. Across the street, a few shops did some business, but the neighborhood was peaceful and calm.

WHILE I WAS busy with housework one day, a faint, yet unmistakable, voice called my name from the outside. Curi-ous, I hurried down the steps to the side door, looked back to the garage, and saw my mother parked there. She looked like she was crying, so I raced to her car and saw the tears flowing down her cheeks.

"Mom, what's wrong?" I asked with deep concern.

She said she had become disoriented and couldn't find her way back home. When she said that, it felt like my heart skipped a beat.

It was almost impossible for my mother to get lost in the city, since she knew every corner like the back of her hand. To avoid having me lead her back to their house, she asked me to give her time to calm down. After we discussed things that distracted her from the current situation, she said she felt better. I hoped that would help her relax. Seeing her like that crushed me. As she pulled away, I watched, praying that God would keep her safe and help her find her way home.

I called my sister and told her what had happened. We determined that the incident was the onset of Alzheimer's disease. After she told me about the disease, I researched it and came to understand it more thoroughly. Knowing my mother was losing her memory dominated my thoughts and ate away at my emotions for months.

Why is this happening to one of the most kindhearted people on Earth, who holds God's spirit within hers? I wondered. Aware that our bodies are imperfect, I dared not blame God for her condition, but I asked Him to comfort her in her time of need.

Living in my rental house alone had its advantages, but eventually, the loneliness became annoying. I needed to interact with others, so I did what I knew and went to the club one night. My one-stop socializing trip allowed me to loosen up, meet people, and make friends and associates. I was even introduced to a contact who sold marijuana.

Now, my move was complete.

My new friends and I began spending time together, usually on the weekends or sometimes during the week after I got off work. Most received assistance and didn't have a job, and we caught up with those who did when their shifts ended. Each day, riding around the city, smoking in the car, and drinking and smoking at our destination held a new adventure with a familiar theme. There was a possibility for an attraction to be shared with one new friend, but subdued interest held out hopefully with each day that passed. Toby was my height and about my weight. I was drawn to their long, curly jet-black hair and dark-chocolate skin.

Time revealed that the feeling was mutual, and we became the couple in our group of friends. Usually, four of us gathered. Sometimes there was a fifth, but they hung out with us only periodically. During one of our gatherings, Toby sat next to me and began a cryptic conversation. After I asked them to clarify, they pulled some rocks out of their pocket. I did a double-take, looking at them and then back at their hand. I had left that behind me two years before, and now it had come back into my life by way of an offer.

They asked if I wanted to smoke it like them, but I refused. The only way I smoked it was with my weed.

Now that my initiation into their little circle's inner sanctum was complete, I was obligated to drive them to purchase their product and then to where they chose to smoke afterward. We occasionally visited stores in the local mall with our female companion. An expert shoplifter, she sometimes stole items—a practice in which I regrettably joined—to sell or trade for the rock when the money ran low. I sat in the car with my partner, her, and another friend many times. They smoked the rock in their tools as I smoked my primo joint; they seemed to enjoy their experience more than I did. They continued to ask me to smoke it like them, but I refused until one day, I didn't.

The overwhelming sensation was completely new to me and unlike anything I had ever experienced. I craved to repeat the sensation as soon as possible. I found myself wishing to enjoy smoking the rock like that every day. Before I knew it, my preference shifted from marijuana to rock, and I became fully immersed in the pursuit, acquisition, and use of this substance.

At first, we traveled to various parts of the city, but I soon found places near me that sold it. One place was an apartment complex across the street from the community building. That meant I didn't have to drive around the city anymore. It also opened the door for sellers to come to me since I lived so close. They came when I called because they knew I had a job and was a veteran with monetary benefits.

Most of the activity occurred during the evening, late into the night, and sometimes into the morning sunlight. My friend and I began to grow apart; they had become overwhelmed by the activity and popularity my house had drawn. I began to acquire a larger circle of associates—people needing somewhere to smoke their substance in comfortable surroundings. I had the entertainment, the kitchen to cook in when we got hungry, and the space to lie down and sleep in if necessary. So, after a suppressed exchange, Toby and I went our separate ways.

Unexpected Consequence

The loneliness that once haunted me had dispersed as my location transformed into a hub of activity. The constant coming and going of individuals created a lively atmosphere, with people engaged in the rituals of smoking, drinking, and experiencing the pleasures that came with smoking rock daily. My home had seamlessly progressed into a gathering spot within the neighborhood, a sanctuary where one could freely indulge in their chosen activities without the fear of judgment or imposition.

As substance abuse addicts, we all did whatever our desires demanded and whatever it took to obtain it. It was evident from who and how many people came through my door that this substance had captured those less fortunate and destroyed others' lives. It was, nevertheless, a rock-fueled world of debauchery, scandal, and expression that united us all. The interesting part was that it was my house, and I was responsible for running the operation smoothly. This meant turning people away when necessary.

HAVING BECOME a familiar customer to several distributors, I asked one of them if they wanted to use my house as their location to avoid exposure where they were. The little apartment saw a lot of activity, and its bedroom saw even more. It was also a way to ensure that rock was always available. Much to my delight, they agreed, and that's when I began smoking every day. Make no mistake; they made me pay for everything they gave me, except for what I charged them for renting the space to do business. In addition, anyone who purchased and wanted to smoke there had to pay the house with part of their substance, and I smoked that as well.

Eventually, my smoking got the best of my finances, and I began to neglect some of my responsibilities. The light bill came due, and I scrambled to get it paid, even asking one of the dealers to help, which they did because they wanted to keep the lights on. They had grown accustomed to my spot. Unfortunately, I did not receive the same assistance when my car note came due, and the bank eventually repossessed it. That was a problem because Mom was the cosigner, and the repossession would show on her credit report. We discussed it, and she was disappointed in me. But I promised to resume paying the car note until it was paid off.

A while after the operation was underway, a revelation

was made during a conversation. One of the dealers who had set up shop in my house was my high school partner's nephew. After we established that connection, their treatment of me became more favorable, and they gave me credit whenever I asked. Eventually, the word got to my ex-partner that their nephew was selling at my location, and one day, they decided to visit my house.

I was shocked to see Trey when I opened the door. After they spoke to me, I let them in. Then they talked to their nephew, purchased some rocks, and began smoking. Trey's visits became more regular, and they seemed to show a renewed interest in me. At the time, so many people came through my house daily that my time was consumed by entertaining and monitoring the activities. Some caught my attention, and with some of them, I shared in the expression. I barely noticed their pursuit. Their visits decreased after a while because the interest was not reciprocated.

Over time, new customers, including a former house madam, joined the regulars. After visiting for a short while, she began trying to control the activities in my house. The dealers stayed out of the impending disagreement, not wanting to ruffle her feathers, so I was unsure how to confront her and set her straight. After discussing the predicament with a select few people, I finally mustered up the courage to face up to her. Consequently, I let my anger get the best of me and acted out physically.

It was winter; the temperatures must have been in the twenties, and a moderate layer of snow blanketed the ground. Standing at the top of the side doorsteps, she said something that made me snap. I rushed into my bedroom, which she had taken over, grabbed all her stuff, and headed for the side door. While I was throwing her bags out into the snow, she grabbed my arm and yelled, "Stop!"

On reflex, I took my right hand across my body, grabbed her by the arm she was holding me with, yanked her grip off me, threw her out into the snow with her belongings, turned around, went inside, and slammed the door behind me.

The feeling of empowerment swelled in my chest as I returned upstairs. Everyone had shocked looks on their faces. They hadn't expected that of me. They did not know much about me except what they saw of me in those surroundings, but what they saw that night was me taking back control of my house.

Business returned to normal, only sometimes, the dealers could not be at my home. So we had to walk to the apartment or somewhere else to score. On two occasions, my choice to be the runner turned out to be ill-fated.

WHILE CONVERSING with another guest after we had run out of money and couldn't get credit, they devised a plan to get some. It would take both of us for it to work, and they began laying out the details. There was a corner store down the street. Usually, only one person operated it during the day, so we thought that raiding it should be easy.

"I'll draw the clerk's attention, asking questions about the bottles of wine at the back of the store. Then you come in, open the cash register, which is by the front door, and snatch the money. We'll both run out together," the planner said with confidence.

It sounded like a foolproof strategy, and I needed to get high, so I agreed to proceed with the mission.

When we reached the store, the planner entered and drew the clerk's attention away from the front door by starting a conversation. Peering around the doorframe, I watched as they walked back to the cooler full of wine. When the clerk's back was turned, I slipped in and tried to open the register, but it wouldn't open. I panicked and became frantic, pushing all the knobs and trying to get the drawer to open. This alerted the clerk, who turned to see me and started yelling for me to stop. That's when the planner started beating him on the head with a bottle of wine.

We both ran from the store, both going in separate directions. Our escape had to be spontaneous and swift. The clerk had pulled out his pistol from behind the counter and was prepared to start shooting.

I ran straight across the street. When I stopped one block away, I was in an empty lot with overgrown grass and weeds that were tall enough for me to crouch down and not be seen. It reminded me of my training in the military when we had to escape and evade the enemy.

The faint sound of police sirens in the distance was nearing my location. I figured the clerk must have called them or pressed a panic button.

As I watched through the tall grass, the police arrived at the store and began speaking with the clerk, who met them at the door. My heart was pounding. *Should I move or wait until they leave?* I wondered. I couldn't make up my mind. The police finally walked into the store, and that's when I made my move. I ran as fast as my frail, malnourished, drug-ravaged body would go.

When I reached the house, I couldn't hold back, telling everyone about my experience. They all hung on my every word. Their faces revealed their disbelief that I had tried something so daring.

On another occasion, while I was walking down the sidewalk from the apartment complex one night, a police car pulled up beside me near the empty lot next to my home. An officer got out and walked toward me, instructing me to put my hands in the air. Since I was holding rocks in my hand, I threw them into the empty lot beside my house when I raised my arms.

It was dark, so I'm sure they didn't see the rocks fly out of my hand and into the empty lot. As they frisked me, they told me why they were doing so. Someone had reported a lot of suspected drug activity in the area, and they were on patrol for any perpetrators. I suppose I fit the description. Fortunately, they didn't find anything on me. These were, however, only precursors to what would happen not long after I threw the house madam out.

Two people and the dealer were watching television in the living room, and two other people besides me were enjoying the calming atmosphere that was created by Madam's absence. Suddenly, a loud knock on the front door startled all of us. It was followed by someone yelling, "Police! Open up!"

I ran to the door to open it, but the dealer told me not to. The dealer, who had the product in the open, hurried to stash it away in some artificial plants.

The police knocked a third time, saying they were breaking the door down and coming in.

I immediately ran back toward the dining room with the two other people. When I reached it, the police burst through the door. Everybody in the house was lying on their stomachs with their hands behind their heads. We knew what came next. The police extensively searched the home but could not locate the product. However, they did find the tools we used. That would be significant when we reached the police station and were booked into custody.

After placing the restraints on us, they stood us up and explained the reason for the raid. The officer mentioned that someone had called 911 to report a White lady being forcibly taken into a rock house, and I immediately recognized it as Madam's act of revenge. They escorted us out of the house and into the waiting police van; fortunately, it was late at night, reducing the chances of public visibility. While they didn't charge me with kidnapping or possession of a controlled substance, I did face charges for possession of criminal tools since they'd discovered them in my house.

Once the legal formalities concluded, they ushered me into one of the holding cells, pushing me through the entrance and slamming the heavy metal bar door shut behind me. That huge door clicking shut was the most horrific sound, sending shivers throughout my body as I walked toward an unoccupied seat. The holding cell was crowded; I was sharing space with others arrested for various offenses, some wearing expressions of sorrow. Others retained a sense of defiance in their demeanor and conversations.

I spent four days in jail with people who had committed worse offenses than I had. It was the most degrading experience, and when my court date arrived, I was hoping they would let me go on my own recognizance. To my profound disappointment, my impending release required that I do more jail time and perform community service or enter the drug recovery program at the veterans' hospital.

Of course, I chose the latter, and my ride to the hospital arrived the next day. Walking away from that police station and jail, I vowed never to smoke that substance ever. I would not let it take away my freedom again. It wasn't like my stay with the Germans; they had restrained me, booked me, and then locked me away, which was the worst feeling of my life.

We stopped by my house to gather whatever I might need for the duration of the program. While doing so, I started searching for the rock in the artificial plants. After a hurried search, I found nothing, but then I thought the dealer must have returned and retrieved the product. I found the side door ajar, so either the dealer or someone else had broken in during my time away and found it. So I abandoned my search. Disappointed that I didn't find anything, I finished gathering my belongings, returned to the car, and headed for the VA hospital in the big city.

What would I have done with it if it had been there when I looked for it?

Our recovery program was housed in the now-defunct outpatient clinic in the big city's suburb. Upon arriving at the hospital, I encountered sympathetic staff who efficiently assisted me with in-processing procedures. The recovery program would last thirty days and involved speakers sharing their stories about addiction, recovery principles, twelve-step practices, and other life-management tools to help us regain our dignity.

The agenda also focused on helping veterans find employment by providing interview coaching, resume preparation, and an in-house vocational program. Some departments in the hospital offered veterans employment during their recovery. The goal was to help each person establish a stable employment record and secure a job within the VA health care system or elsewhere after they completed the program.

When they presented the opportunity to me, I immediately chose the Information Technology Department. I had an intense, inherent yearning to work with computers. So they created a position called computer specialist. My focus was desktop computers, but I was also called on to perform other duties in other areas of the field. I messed up only when they asked me to rewire connections in the communications closet, and they never asked me to do it again. I didn't like working with wires anyway.

The recovery program administrators allowed us to look for a place to stay at the end of our program, and my search ended with an apartment within walking distance of the hospital. On one of the main throughways in the city, the eight-story brick building stood on the corner among others with the same construction and some newer structures within the college district.

My apartment was on the seventh floor and was furnished with nicely kept furniture. The view was fantastic. On one occasion, a fire occurred in an apartment on the first floor, and everyone had to use the smoke-filled stairwell to escape. That was a scary situation; we couldn't see, and we coughed as we ran down the stairs through the exit to the outside. After I arrived outdoors, I caught my breath and thought, *I will never live in a high-rise again.* Luckily, the fire didn't cause extensive damage, and we were allowed to return to our apartments after the fire had been extinguished.

THE YEAR WAS 1990, and the World Wide Web was in its infancy; it was referred to as The Bulletin Board, and desktop computers had recently become available to big businesses and organizations. Distribution factories shipped large units and individual computer parts to the hospital, and my job was to put the unit together and prepare it for use. Hospitals installed them to replace the workstations staff used to connect to the main computer. A desktop computer made creating documents and communicating with the hospital's data infrastructure more efficient.

My two mentors taught me everything they knew about computers. When we received the computer parts, they showed me how to assemble them and install the Disk Operating System (DOS) software and the now-famous Microsoft Windows Operating System software, Versions 2 and 3.0. After ensuring all the software worked as it should, I took it to prospective individuals, familiarized them with the unit and software, and performed maintenance whenever they encountered technical problems.

I became highly skilled in my job duties over time, which led to my transfer to the main hospital. There, they tasked me with overseeing the installation and management of hundreds of computers. Despite the daunting nature of the job, I rose to the challenge and impressed everyone around me. I even received compliments from secretaries, administrative assistants, section chiefs, and administrators. After I had been at the hospital for three years, they acknowledged me as the employee of the month. Staying clean, living wise and healthy, and being dedicated to my job had rewards, and many people in the hospital came to know me and respect who I was.

Many of my coworkers began encouraging me to utilize my veterans' education benefits to further my knowledge of computers. Since the field was new and advancing quickly, I thought it would be beneficial, so I signed up to attend the nearby community college. I chose to take computer science and English 101 as my course study. Unfortunately, my job required much attention, and late-night work-related activities began to take a toll on my attendance and performance in class, so I reluctantly decided to quit.

MY POPULARITY SOARED when the hospital's Black History Month recognition took place. I was a member of the hospital employee choir, and the hospital asked us for ideas they could incorporate into the program that year. I offered to write an original play, and my request was approved.

When the program day arrived, all nonessential personnel came to see the production. Every actor in the play performed exceptionally well and delivered their lines without error. When we bowed to signal the conclusion, we received a standing ovation. In the following days, countless people spoke of how much they enjoyed the celebration, with many congratulating me personally.

My life had changed entirely by the end of my fourth year of employment. I worked for the government and lived near my workplace; my health remained stable; I did not drink or use drugs for four years; I kept my promise to pay the car note my mom had cosigned for, and I had no social distractions. My life had become perfectly functional again.

The last statement isn't exactly true. While I wore success and professionalism well on the outside, the lack of personal interaction with people outside work made me lonely.

It wasn't unusual for someone to catch my attention when I was working in such a large hospital with people coming and going in all directions. While crossing the hospital's main lobby one day, my attraction spotted bowlegs; loose, curly jet-black hair; and neatly shaven caramel-cream skin. They were standing at the police station, asking the guard a question. As I approached them, their attention turned to me, and they asked for directions to their destination. I offered to show them, and we conversed as we walked, sharing some information about ourselves along the way. We exchanged numbers when we reached where they were going and promised to stay in touch.

Upon receiving their call, I felt excited and promptly began preparing for their visit. When we were in each other's company again, our conversation flowed smoothly, as if we had been long-time friends. There was an obvious mutual attraction between us, and I took the initiative to express my feelings, which they reciprocated.

After several more intensely engaging visits, I invited them to move in. We were a handsome, happy couple, getting compliments from everyone we knew. Now, my life was perfect—almost too good to be true.

There's a saying that you never really know someone until you've lived with them, which became disturbingly accurate in this instance. Although initially charismatic, their behavior became problematic several months after we moved in together.

When confronted, they did tell the truth, even presenting the rock to me as a peace offering. They had caught me in a moment of anguish and emotional turmoil, and I was willing to do whatever it would take to stay close to them.

I took the tool, put it to my mouth, and inhaled. Instantly, four years of addiction recovery went up in smoke.

DURING THE FIRST few months of my fifth year of employment, no one in the hospital knew of or suspected my use of rock until I began losing weight and coming to work late. It was never explicitly mentioned, except one friend noticed and asked out of concern. By then, my partner and I had experienced a falling-out due to their inappropriate behavior during our last shared smoking session. Once again, my heart broke, and my addiction was raging. All this made me feel like the darkness was swallowing me. The despair was overwhelming, and I couldn't take it anymore.

While they watched television in the living room, I went into the bathroom, opened the cabinet, and removed a bottle of my sleep medication. I unscrewed the cap, poured some in the palm of my hand, turned the water on, threw the pills into my mouth, leaned under the faucet, and swallowed them with water. I returned to the living room to watch television as if things were normal. As the drowsiness gradually increased, my eyes began to close, and my thoughts faded into the shadows.

My odd behavior caught their attention, and they immediately grabbed and started shaking me while calling my name. I could barely open my eyes, and my body was limp. I did not try to stay awake.

My career had ended before it had the chance to become prominent, my partner was promiscuous, and I had ruined four years of sobriety. What was there to live for?

Drifting farther down into the darkness, I heard the

faint sound of that person's voice as they called for the ambulance. I didn't care. I just wanted the relentless torment to end. I wanted to go to sleep forever.

The paramedics arrived within what seemed to be a matter of minutes. When they picked me up off the floor and placed me on the stretcher, I was nonresponsive but could still hear. The paramedics kept yelling, "Stay with me! Come on, stay with me!" while tapping me on my face and strapping me to the stretcher.

None of that mattered. I was on the stretcher. Now I could sleep.

When they lifted the stretcher, a sudden outburst from that individual's lips jolted me from the depths of my self-loathing.

"What about your mother?" they yelled.

My eyes shot open in response. *I can't do this to my mother,* I thought. *Could that have been God calling out to me, using the treacherous mouth of this individual to pull me out of the darkness?*

I got only a shadowy glimpse of their presence as the paramedics ushered me toward the door. I never wanted to see that person again. The paramedics rushed me down two flights of stairs, through the apartment complex's front door, and into the waiting ambulance. They then raced against time, relaying their anticipated arrival by the radio to the nearest emergency room.

The ambulance doors flung open when we reached the hospital. They quickly removed me from the vehicle and immediately rushed me toward the nearest examination room. Inside, the medical staff had meticulously readied themselves for a case of amphetamine overdose, ensuring all necessary tools were readily available. Though I remained lethargic, I was alert enough as they explained the need to induce nausea to expel the pills from my stomach. I couldn't disagree with the proposal. It was a profoundly humiliating moment, but I became more alert and responsive afterward.

With their immediate action taken, they promptly notified the VA hospital and apprised them of my suicide attempt. Shortly afterward, an ambulance transported me to the VA hospital, where they placed me in the intensive care unit.

As I lay motionless with a tube in my nose, listening to the monotonous rhythm of the heart monitoring machine, the reality of what I had done began to take hold. Several coworkers and other hospital staff came to see me out of concern for my well-being. For them to see me like that was the most humiliating moment of my life.

WHEN THEY DISCHARGED ME, I returned to my apartment to find that my enabler had gathered all their belongings and left. That relieved my anticipation of having to see and deal with them again when they released me from the hospital. The apartment was a disaster, but I couldn't tackle it until I regained strength. I grabbed a bite to eat, promptly went into my bedroom, and fell asleep.

The next morning, my supervisor reassured me over a call that my job was secure and encouraged me to return to work the coming week if possible. Grateful for the assurance, I thought, *Thank God. I still have my job!*

Despite some lingering weariness, I resumed my duties and gradually returned to my usual self, though not 100 percent. Colleagues welcomed me back with warm smiles and kind words, their support boosting my confidence to persist.

During a hallway conversation, a coworker shared news about a new VA employee benefit that had recently become available for eligible veterans. The VA had created an early-retirement program for employees facing medical challenges. Intrigued, I quickly researched the details and found that my HIV status made me eligible. Considering this, I decided to use it as a compelling reason for early retirement, hoping for a favorable response to my request. My job performance may have improved after the incident, but the memory of my near-successful suicide attempt still lingered in my mind.

One day, while I was intensely focused on repairing a computer, someone from the personnel office called. They informed me that the VA had approved my request for early retirement. I froze momentarily; I could not believe they had accepted my concerns. When our conversation concluded, I stood up from my desk, raised my arms high, and thanked God.

My life was back on track. But it was a remarkable feeling this time because I no longer had to work to get paid. This development was a benefit I hadn't expected to utilize so soon; nevertheless, it felt like the smart thing to do because the offer presented itself.

In the following weeks, after signing the retirement papers, I utilized some of my free time to look for old friends. The Internet had finally evolved into its preliminary infrastructure, and I used it to locate an old army interest who lived in Queens, New York.

WHEN I HAD BEGUN training for the Airborne Corps at Fort Bragg, this person was one of our training instructors. On that first day, when we dismounted from the truck, they guided us to the designated formation area. As our eyes met, with their face partly concealed beneath the distinctive instructor's hat, my attraction was immediate. Concentrating on the tasks at hand could sometimes be challenging.

Following the conclusion of our training program, we remained in close contact, frequently visiting and spending time with each other. Eventually, we became a committed couple. Yet, as life unfolds, nothing remains constant, and this premise holds within military service duties. My reassignment sent me to Germany, and they went to another state. We lost contact after that.

When I reached out all those years later, we caught up on everything since our last time together, including their job and workplace. They had found employment as a prison security guard. I found that type of employment intriguing and asked for more information. Aware of my situation—the retirement, not my past troubles—they invited me to move there and said they would help me apply for a position where they worked. By the end of our conversation, I was so thoroughly excited about moving to New York that I wasted no time preparing. When the day of my bus departure arrived, I caught a taxi to the bus terminal, boarded my bus, and was off to The Big Apple.

The bus ride to New York made me more anticipatory than the one from California had. This was primarily because moving to a bustling city and reuniting with my long-time friend Sam made my expectations almost unbearable. The sight of towering buildings as we approached the inner city left me amazed. The term *skyscrapers* is fitting, as the tops of some buildings were barely visible from the ground.

When we pulled into the terminal, Sam was waiting with a big smile. They helped me put my belongings in the car, and we headed for their home in Queens.

The apartment was situated on the fifth floor of a high-rise complex. It was a charming one-bedroom with a generously sized living room, a compact dining area, and a practical kitchen. It was in one of several similarly constructed buildings that stretched along the entire street. The surrounding area was populated by additional apartment buildings and small enterprises, with a partially obscured church nestled among the trees at the end of the adjacent block. During the day, the foot traffic was moderate, while at night, I could hear the distant sound of the subway train's brakes grinding to a stop.

∽

OUR REUNION WAS JOYOUS. Being in their presence again, seeing their face, hearing their voice, and expressing myself to them made me feel like, this time, this relationship was going to flourish.

My friend worked during the day, which allowed me to survey the immediate neighborhood. I even went into the city several times, looking for temporary employment until I received word on my application submission. It took a while to hear back, so on one of my outings, I stopped at the church because we needed assistance to feed both of us properly.

The church gave me groceries and a monetary gift to help with bills needing attention, with a stipulation attached. When I found ample employment, I would pay the church back their donation so they could put it with other funds and make it available for others in need. It was a gracious act for them to aid someone not previously known to them—a stranger whom their spirits chose to help. I was so grateful and honored that they found it within themselves to help my friend and me.

On another occasion, it was stuffy in the apartment, so I struck out to get some air and survey more of the surroundings. When I left the apartment building, I crossed the street and walked along the sidewalk to the next street corner. As I prepared to cross the street, I looked to my left and then glanced to my right. That's when I saw several people standing around talking halfway down the block. As I continued looking, two people exchanged something, and one of them promptly left the group and disappeared into the apartment building across the street.

Every alarm, whistle, and red flag erupted in my mind—an outcry of warning signals that left no room for doubt about what I had just witnessed. Simultaneously, my stomach growled and cramped, forcing me to bend slightly at the waist. It was an instinctive reaction, reminiscent of the anticipatory physical responses seen in a rock addict about to indulge. It sometimes even triggers gastrointestinal distress. Summoning all my willpower, I suppressed these turbulent reactions and pressing thoughts, then continued with my neighborhood discovery. However, an unforgettable seed had been sown, and the disturbing memory of that scene clung to me for days.

Inevitably, the haunting recall of that interaction began to overpower my attempts to suppress it. One day, while my friend worked, I confronted the situation head-on. My suspicions were confirmed when I reached the location. I encountered a small group of individuals across the street from the adjacent apartment building. One posed the pivotal question before I approached them.

"What are you looking for?" they asked.

With a portion of the church money still in my possession, I had the means to procure the rock. But I needed the necessary equipment to smoke it with. My only recourse was to find someone with the appropriate tool and share their apparatus with them. Fortunately, someone who had also just purchased offered to let me use theirs, proposing we go to their secluded spot together to indulge.

I followed them as we entered the apartment building and ascended the stairs that led to the rooftop. As we climbed, they revealed their challenging circumstances and explained that this rooftop served as their dwelling. When we finally pushed open the door to the roof, an awe-inspiring sight greeted us.

The evening sky was magnificent; the sun had begun to set with its radiant glow as the faint image of the moon rose through the clouds in the distance. This perfect weather made me wonder how they managed during less hospitable conditions. Their personal belongings were arranged in an orderly way around their neatly spread-out blanket, which they used as a place to sit and a makeshift bed.

We met and smoked often; they even became an unofficial protector, expressing concern for my well-being. During one conversation, they asked about my origins and where I'd come from. When I told them, they asked if my mother was still alive, to which I answered yes. They then told me to leave New York and return home to my mother.

"This isn't where you should be," they expressed.

That exchange made me wonder whether this person was an instrument God was using to warn me of impending danger.

After my protector friend and I had met up to smoke a few days later, I noticed that Sam, who had returned home early, appeared visibly troubled when I walked through the door. When I inquired about the cause of their distress, they launched into an impassioned speech about substance use, the excessive quantities consumed, and the individuals who partook in it. They told me their brother had grappled with the addiction, resulting in a tragic outcome. Sam said there were echoes of that struggle in my behavior.

Then Sam retrieved a tightly secured carrying case containing a forty-five caliber handgun, a standard issue for prison security guards. With a stern tone, they warned me that dire consequences would follow if I ever considered stealing anything to feed my habit.

Profound fear consumed me as their menacing words pierced my spirit, warning me of my situation's perilous turn. Their ominous threat of fatal violence offered no alternative but to leave promptly. *Could this be the danger spoken of by my protector?* I wondered.

Once again, I sought the unwavering support of my sister—a beacon of reassurance in the darkest of times.

I set out on a subway journey toward the bus terminal. When we arrived, I swiftly located the check-in desk, secured my ticket, and bid a bittersweet farewell to The Big Apple, my dreams unfulfilled. Alongside my emotional baggage of another failed relationship and relapse, I carried the weight of not only an unpaid debt to the church but guilt for using a portion of it for drugs, a lingering burden I have had on my conscience for years.

5

THE PLIGHT

Functional Rehabilitation

My unexpected early return home surprised my parents, who still greeted me warmly, without judgment, and with open arms. They grasped the gravity of my situation and genuinely empathized with my willingness to return to the recovery program. During our conversation, they shared some of their life choices with me. Their words encouraged and reinforced my confidence in what I had chosen to do.

Getting into the hospital recovery program immediately was the obstacle. Routine intake procedures and admission could take hours, sometimes days or weeks. Nevertheless, I had a long-thought-out, foolproof strategy for prompt entry. For that to happen, my plan required a mode of transportation to get there. Thankfully, my parents graciously offered to drive me, sealing their unwavering support and commitment to my well-being.

We departed for the VA clinic in the big city suburb the following morning.

I bid them goodbye when we arrived because I knew my plan would work. When I turned and walked through the main door, I crossed paths with a nurse on her way to attend to her duties. Taking the initiative to get her attention, I expressed the emotional turmoil I grappled with. I continued by sharing vital information about my past suicide attempt and the resurgence of those painful memories revisiting me.

In response to my evident distress, the compassionate nurse swiftly guided me to the emergency room, where they promptly initiated observation and monitoring. At the same time, recognizing the situation's urgency, she reached out to a mental health specialist on the ward, ensuring I would receive the specialized care and attention I needed.

My ongoing struggle with this substance had taken a heavy toll, resulting in early retirement from my job, a significant decline in physical health, the loss of personal possessions, a severe blow to my self-esteem, temporary incarceration, and a brush with a near-fatal outcome. This addiction is a formidable adversary, similar to my attempts to quit smoking cigarettes, yet more unrelenting. Like the persistent craving for a cigarette, even after cessation, the relentless yearning for this substance can reach an overwhelmingly unquenchable intensity. Given the circumstances, the primary focus now had to shift to safeguarding my mental well-being.

They placed me in the only available spot in the mental health ward, and it was disconcerting to witness the daily mental battles endured by my fellow veterans. Among them were various degrees of afflictions, with a minority grappling with more severe cognitive challenges. The dedicated staff conducted numerous assessments and tests to gauge my condition, and I started a regular regimen of mental health counseling. My stay in that ward was a soul-stirring reminder of my good fortune in grappling solely with addiction and its effects while maintaining a relatively stable cognitive state of mind.

My transition into the addiction recovery program flowed seamlessly, involving a simple move within the hospital. This marked the beginning of yet another journey back to sobriety, a path I was ashamed to be walking once more but needed to walk again. Returning so swiftly was humbling, and I recognized that this was the sole means of halting the grip of addiction from further ravaging my life.

At the end of the program, I had made friends and regained the encouragement and recovery tools I needed to go out and try life again.

~

AFTER RETURNING TO MY PARENTS' home and purchasing a car without my mother's signature this time, I struck out looking for a job. Offering my clerical experience, I secured a job at a small income tax and accounting firm. My primary duties included handling office documentation and in-house correspondence. Occasionally, I also prepared documents for client review.

After I had been working at this job for several months, my car started having mechanical issues that would have cost too much to fix. Taking this into consideration, I decided to use the money that would have been spent on repairs as a down payment on another vehicle. Fortunately, the son of the accounting company's owner had a used car dealership, and she was able to put in a good word for me. I went to the dealership and purchased an old used station wagon. They talked me into it, and in no time, I drove it off the lot.

There was, however, no positive aspect to this acquisition. The overpowering smell of gasoline permeated the car during my ride home. Anger swelled within me; it was evident they had sold me a lemon. I told my parents when I reached home, who expressed their concerns and explained my options. Bringing myself to face the owner or her son after that defrauding transaction was out of the question. I never returned to work after that. Eventually, I used the car as a trade-in for something more suitable.

During my subsequent job search, I used my veteran status and prior security work history to obtain an interview with a local security company. Sitting in the waiting area, I started mentally gearing up for the impending meeting. Unfortunately, the time was insufficient because I was unprepared for the person who walked through the door to conduct the interview. This individual was tall with bowlegs, a healthy cinnamon-colored complexion, a contagious smile, and an engaging demeanor.

We left an indelible impression on each other during that encounter. Yet my primary concern was the impression that I had made.

It was positive, as I received the news that I would start working the following week. While an immediate attraction to my soon-to-be supervisor sparked within me, I decided to convey my friendly personality and keep our relationship professional. As we continued to interact, it became evident that we shared similar personality traits, including a particular sense of humor. So, searching for and finding this job allowed me to secure employment with the added benefit of a close friendship.

During their occasional visits to my duty sites, they sometimes spoke of our initial encounter and reflected on their first impressions of me while engaging in casual conversation. They often mentioned how I carried myself as a former military person. They could tell the moment they saw me. The recurring joke in these reminiscences centered around the vehicle I drove when I first began working.

The running gag was about my car's persistent gas line leak, which led to an overpowering scent of gasoline that penetrated the trailing vehicle and made everybody in that car cough. I was already aware of the foul odor. Though funny, it was also embarrassing.

MY EXPECTATIONS around being a security guard with this company were quite different from the duties I had performed at my other security job. While some assignments echoed aspects of my previous role, this job extended beyond the confines of discount stores. One notable location was a massive warehouse where we were responsible for hourly patrols of the premises during the night.

Between those intervals, I maximized my downtime at the security post by delving into the world of books. At that moment, my preferred reading material was the book series titled *The Destroyer*, with Remo Williams as the central character. It is worth highlighting that this book series was eventually adapted into a film and television series. The production was executed with remarkable skill and superior craftsmanship.

After a few months of my employment, the county board of education called on our company to provide security for a strike at the local schools. This was a welcome change for all of us, and we looked forward to our new assignment with much anticipation. The job was a cakewalk. We strolled through the school building, reminiscing about our school days. We stood outside and observed the protesters, ensuring no one attempted to cause damage to the premises. They even provided lunches to make our stay more hospitable.

DISCOVERING this company and forging a friendship with its head supervisor came with its advantages, one of which extended beyond the boundaries of employment. As I continued my term with the company for several months, the moment arrived again for me to transition away from my parents' home.

Unexpectedly, fate smiled upon me, as my supervisor's sibling owned a house merely four streets away from my family's church. Upon seeing the property, I formed an instant connection with the one-story, one-bedroom cabin-style home, which I affectionately referred to as my little bungalow. This fortunate circumstance not only provided me with a new residence but also facilitated connections with other members of my supervisor's family. My supervisor's mother even became a good friend and asked me to babysit her grandchild a few times.

Once again, my life gained worth, purpose, stability, and the comforting shelter of a roof over my head, along with the luxury of being able to walk to my family's church for services.

Recuperative Expectations

Days turned into weeks, weeks flowed into months, and months into years. During that time, my benefits increased, and the biweekly employment pay was the perfect supplement. Everything was sailing smoothly until, one fateful day, my body delivered an unmistakable and alarming warning about my health.

The day could not have been more ideal for some house maintenance. The weather had been consistently warm and rain-free for several days. With this reasonable weather in mind, I tackled some cleaning chores in the house and basement. An unexpected dizziness washed over me as I concentrated on collecting unwanted items and sweeping away the debris. Initially, I attributed it to physical exertion, so I pressed on with my task.

Rather than decreasing, my imbalance grew increasingly pronounced as I continued my work. The dizziness overtook me completely while I attempted to ascend the stairs to the main floor, leading to a trip and fall. The intensity of the dizziness was puzzling, leaving me confused about its cause. Regardless of the reason, it became abundantly clear that I needed to seek immediate medical attention at a hospital for a proper diagnosis of this sudden ailment.

After the fall, I took some time to gather myself. Then I attempted to change my clothes, a task compounded by the dizziness, which made it far more intricate and challenging than I had initially anticipated. Once ready, I got into the car and drove myself to the emergency room.

After performing several tests, the medical team determined that I had experienced a mild stroke. They could not believe I had driven in that condition. By that point, the effects had begun to manifest on the right side of my body.

When the oxygen tube and heart monitor were no longer needed, they discharged me to the physical therapy ward to work on my paralysis. When I had regained sufficient agility, I was sent home with specific physical therapy instructions aimed at helping me regain complete control of my right side. Fortunately, the paralysis was temporary and not all-encompassing. I knew to whom I owed my gratitude. My journey back through recovery began within the hospital after they deemed me fit.

After completing my therapy, I returned to work and faithfully resumed attending recovery meetings, fulfilling my promise to myself and, subsequently, my parents. In addition, I received a request from our church family to assist with installing and maintaining desktop computers for the church school's students, a task I regarded as honorable. I did my best to perform satisfactorily; unfortunately, timing and availability became issues, and I was unable to continue providing support.

During my attendance at recovery meetings, I observed people engaging in lively conversations, sharing laughter, and forming bonds of friendship. However, as a newcomer to these gatherings, I had not established personal connections within the recovery rooms. One individual did attract my interest—someone who also frequented my home group. This person seized every opportunity to capture my attention, making their presence known through subtle conversations or handshakes whenever circumstances allowed.

They tell us not to have relationships within two years after beginning our recovery, but I don't think that rule was enforced. Despite their obvious good looks—a head full of thick, loose, long, curly, jet-black hair and a healthy milk-chocolate complexion—I continued to ignore their persistent attempts. It was evident that they were fully aware of their attractiveness and that they found me equally appealing, based on how they kept coming at me. After a considerable period of resisting their advances, I eventually grew weary of their determination and relented.

After several weeks of building our connection, I made the hasty decision to inquire whether they would be interested in moving in with me—a choice I would later come to regret.

About a month prior, I'd had to vacate my beloved bungalow, leaving my babysitting and cookout activities behind to move into a larger house just down the street. Moving Randal in was not time-consuming or involved; they only had a few belongings, which should have caught my attention. They also began receiving harassing calls from the person they had just left.

Except for the phone calls, everything appeared harmonious in the beginning. Our relationship flourished, the house felt cozy, and life seemed to go smoothly. Yet I struggled to comprehend why someone who professed affection for me and had gained access to my dwelling to be with me would step out to be with someone else, using a familiar excuse.

What am I doing wrong? I wondered. *Or what am I not doing?*

The true revelation of this person's infidelity became known when I acquired a health affliction that eventually led to a cancer diagnosis.

I knew they had transmitted the disease to me because I

had always remained faithful in my relationships. The first and only exception to my rule occurred when I was stationed at Fort Bragg. On that occasion, my partner unexpectedly returned home early. The other person, who was my best friend at the time, and I did not have the opportunity to conceal our actions. As my partner walked through the apartment, they immediately sensed that someone had been in our bed. Witnessing the pain in their voice and the anguish etched on their face cut deep into my heart. It was then that I made an unwavering vow never to betray the trust of my partners, regardless of the circumstances or the individuals involved.

My relationship with Randal reached the breaking point. I sent them away as I prepared for my hospital stay and the difficult cancer treatment ahead. Cancer affects everyone differently, with some enduring more severe challenges than others. While severe, my chemotherapy treatment also removed a portion of my body hair. But it did not compare to my grueling radiation therapy experience, which resulted in severe third-degree burns on one-fifth of my body. As a result, I spent an extended period in the burn ward, an experience that felt surreal, especially when I woke up one morning to find my medication tube inadvertently pulled out of my arm.

When I questioned the nurse about the tube, she did not respond, leaving me to speculate that she must have removed it. Given the nature of the pain medication, I assumed it might have compelled me to reveal information about myself as I slept that should remain private. With no definitive answer from the nurse, I concluded that this was her justification for removing the tube. As I lay in that hospital bed, enduring excruciating pain and acutely aware of the circumstances that had led me there, an intense and all-encompassing hatred for that individual and the nurse grew within me and remained for months.

About a year or so later, while visiting an organization in the big city for assistance, I pulled into the parking lot and saw Randal standing outside talking to someone. Do you know the intense glare a lion gives its prey before pouncing on it? That's how my face looked; I was ready to take down my prey. My eyes did not look away from them as I slowly exited the car. They hadn't seen me yet, so I purposely walked up behind them and decided to speak when I stood right up next to them.

When Randal turned and saw me, their face dropped like one of those Halloween masks. It worked! I messed their mind up by appearing somewhere they least expected. With a half smile, because I knew I had shocked them to the core, I spoke and continued walking into the building as if not giving them any further acknowledgment. Satisfaction swelled in my chest; it was such an empowering feeling having them see me drive up in a new car, looking good and well-kept. I knew it made an impression. One of regret, I suspect.

A cancer diagnosis was something I had never conceived of, yet here I stand as a survivor. This was undoubtedly a life reprieve, but what had I done to be given such favor? Why did God spare me when countless others suffered and succumbed to this illness? Is there a purpose behind my miraculous healing? These questions dominated my thoughts during and long after my recovery, and they cross my mind even today.

Gradually, I mustered the strength to seek new living arrangements while temporarily staying with a coworker. This was my new lease on life, and I fully embraced this new chapter. My search led to one of the suburbs in the city, where I secured a furnished studio apartment. I adored my charming, modest one-room apartment. It was my first time living in one. Although small, it was comfortable and had all the essentials: a bed, a couch, a chair, a coffee table, a kitchenette, a desk, and a closet.

NESTLED upon several sprawling acres with tall trees to provide shade, the apartment complex presented a remarkable ambiance of seclusion and serenity. As you approached the entrance, a stone plaque proudly displayed the complex's name, and the surrounding lawn and shrubbery were impeccably groomed. Tucked away from the rural road, the location encountered minimal daytime traffic and a peaceful absence of vehicles during the quiet night hours.

I couldn't have stumbled upon a more captivating place to call home, and when evening fell, I might end the day by enjoying the tranquility and scenic beauty of my surroundings. I felt truly blessed to have discovered such an exceptional, attractive location to live in.

I enjoyed being alone because it was a safe and peaceful recovery opportunity. Also, I enjoyed spending most of my free time online. The digital world offered endless entertainment and productivity solutions that I often utilized. Occasionally, I would venture outside, usually going to the local store, which allowed me to explore the nearby neighborhood. The suburb was charming, with its cozy town center just a few blocks away. Aside from the occasional congestion on the intersecting street, traffic flowed smoothly through the heart of the town.

My daily routine became ingrained as the days became weeks, months, and years. A growing yearning for human interaction stirred within me during that time, leaving me feeling increasingly lonely. I had given myself ample time to fully recuperate from the treatment, with only some minor side effects, like skin discoloration from the radiation burns and a slight physical disorder, but otherwise, my health appeared stable. After years of solitary living during my recovery, I turned to the Internet for companionship.

MY SEARCH ENDED in a big city in the southern part of the state with someone who shared my spiritual values, so our connection was immediate. We got to know each other well, speaking on the phone daily. Then, one day, they popped the question. It wasn't about marriage but about coming to live with them. That was music to my ears—the solution to my loneliness predicament and a chance to see and live in the third-largest city in my state. Wasting no time packing my car, I set out for a new life in another big city.

Their appearance stunned me when we finally met face-to-face. They had not shared their struggle, and it was immediately apparent that they were significantly over-weight. The difference in our sizes was striking, with them being taller and twice my size. However, despite this marked difference in physical appearance, I moved into my new living arrangements without passing any judgment. It was too late to address it anyway; I had already arrived with all my earthly belongings. But I found the lack of transparency and truth on Internet dating sites disconcerting, including how people present themselves online. It's like playing Go Fish: reach in and see what you get.

When not working on my computer, I helped my new housemate, Mason, with various tasks as needed. Most household chores had become my daily responsibility, especially considering Mason's health challenges, which limited their activities. Regrettably, this circumstance prevented me from experiencing the city's captivating attractions with them as my guide.

Despite minor interruptions, I achieved noteworthy accomplishments while on the Internet. One of my most memorable achievements was directly connecting with a well-known sports star. While I won't reveal the details of their response, how they acknowledged me was unexpected. Nevertheless, they recognized my efforts to gain distinction among their many fans. As a result, they will probably remember me whenever I interact with their social media posts or tweets.

While out on one of my solo excursions, I made up an excuse to leave the house but was actually going to search for a particular product. In my experience, regardless of the cities I have called home, locating marijuana has always been a matter of knowing the right places to look and blending in when seeking it out.

A small crowd had gathered near the corner convenience store just a few streets away, easily within walking distance of the house. They were engaged in animated conversations while smoking cigarettes, drinking beer, joking, and laughing. While observing them, I couldn't help but feel that one of them might know where I could purchase some marijuana. After a short while, I knew one would, so I pulled alongside them, lowered the passenger window, and inquired.

It was as if I had uttered some enchanting phrase, as one individual swiftly darted ahead of the others and leaned halfway into my car while confirming my request. They enthusiastically informed me that we needed a quick trip to acquire it, motioning that the location was close. Without hesitation, I allowed them to hop into the car, and we set off to our destination.

Usually, when riding with a stranger, particularly someone involved in the sale of drugs, one might encounter an unsettling sense of unease or apprehension. Yet, this ride proved an exception; we conversed as if we had been long-time friends.

When we arrived at the spot, I reluctantly handed them the money, but they wasted no time procuring the product. Upon their return to the car, I gave them their cut, we exchanged phone numbers, and I drove them back to the corner store and dropped them off, gesturing that I would see them again soon.

Over time, we developed a casual friendship. I shared details about where I lived, what I was experiencing, and the feelings I had developed toward them, but we did not discuss that much. My smoking had become a frequent habit, and I found myself unable to confide in anyone about Mason's growing disapproval, which became increasingly problematic. My contact listened when I needed to speak and offered encouragement when handing me my package. At the time, they were the only person I could talk to.

As the sixth month of my relocation rolled around, an unfortunate turn of events occurred. My relationship with Mason deteriorated as my daily marijuana use became more of an issue. The living situation had turned out to be nothing like I had expected, and smoking helped me deal with the dissatisfaction. Additionally, my housemate's mother fell seriously ill. Upon her discharge from the hospital, the plan was to bring her to our house for care. The medical prognosis was bleak, and they had arranged her care, focusing on hospice and not expecting her to survive for long.

Regrettably, I have always struggled with being in the presence of individuals in such dire circumstances. The proximity of those enduring immense suffering and inevitably inching closer to the moment of transition drains my spirit and creates weakness in my composure. Witnessing someone's decline fills me with an overwhelming sense of emptiness that compels me to leave. The sorrow is too intense, and I must excuse myself immediately.

A few miles from the house, an apartment building closer to the bustling downtown community displayed a For Rent sign. The interview process went smoothly, resulting in them handing over the keys on the spot, and I moved in that weekend. Although my decision did not sit well with my friend, I could not bear to be around and witness someone deteriorating and succumbing to their affliction.

It pains me to admit that, in my haste to depart, I failed to consider the emotional and mental impact my absence would have on my housemate. It was only years later that, through a Facebook chat with their best friend, I learned of the profound loss my housemate had suffered due to my leaving. It was compounded by the recent passing of their mother. They died not long after. Despite the certainty of my decision to leave, hearing of their heartbreak and subsequent death left me with a sense of guilt.

~

With my car packed full of my belongings again, I drove into town and moved into the furnished one-bedroom sublevel apartment without anyone's help, which was usually the case.

It was fascinating to look out my front windows and see the sidewalk at eye level, watching legs and feet walking as people passed by. The location was peaceful, on an urban side street, and had everything I needed within walking distance. I was happy with the move.

After a few weeks, I fell back into my daily routine. I spent my time reading articles on the Internet, reacting to them, and occasionally sharing the ones I found interesting. The building where I lived was quiet, and most of the tenants kept to themselves, not revealing anything about their personal lives. I, too, kept to myself and enjoyed the peace and solitude. However, one day, I started feeling something jumping on my skin and crawling on the hairs of my arms.

This went on for days, getting more intense, and the days turned into weeks. It was almost unbearable; it was difficult to concentrate during the day, and I often slept under my covers at night. Eventually, the landlord responded to my complaints and hired exterminators to fumigate the property. As it turned out, my complaint was one among many.

As fate would have it, a new tenant moved into the apartment above mine around the same time, and they promptly disrupted whatever semblance of tranquility remained. The disturbance occurred one night, just one week after their arrival. The unmistakable sounds of intimate moments shared by two individuals in the bedroom directly above me abruptly became a decidedly erotic and intrusive experience.

I had anticipated running into this person, but I needed to figure out how to approach them. The noises I heard were unsettling, and I wished I could get them to stop; it was happening every weekend. On one occasion, I almost saw them as they entered their apartment, but I decided to wait for another chance to confront them, giving me more time to prepare. As I returned from an appointment one day, we ran into each other at the entrance. What I saw left me speechless for a moment.

As they walked past me, I knew I couldn't let the opportunity slip. Summoning the courage to speak was challenging, especially when faced with someone who could be a *GQ* model. With chiseled arms and legs and a chest layered in smooth, chocolate skin, their appearance oozed sensuality, which made it difficult for me to maintain my composure. Despite this, I was proud of myself for speaking up.

Unfortunately, we didn't get along well after that, as they kept having company, and I continued to complain. I had to decide whether to leave or wait for them to move out. But that wouldn't happen, since they had just moved in. So I started searching on the Internet for a new place to stay. After an unsuccessful search for an affordable apartment in the city, I decided that returning home to be around my family and friends would be healthy. It was also exciting when I reconnected with my high school artist friend, Trey, through Facebook during my search.

Even though their page was not regularly active, which was curious, and their picture was obscured, their distinctive facial features were prominent. I was also pleasantly surprised to discover that they still lived in our hometown. When I called the number on their page, to my surprise, they answered. The greeting, to my relief, was cordial, and we began talking as if our questionable past encounters had been wiped away. So, I packed up all my belongings and set out on another relocation journey, hopeful that this move would bring more promise than the last.

IT WAS like experiencing déjà vu, only in reverse. Looking at all the scenery I had passed driving south several months prior, I was now seeing what it looked like from the other side. Again, this drive was tolerable, not too long or short, but I made sure to save time getting to my destination.

When I approached the house, I saw my old high school friend Trey standing outside, ready to greet me. The only thing was, it was not their house; the owner was a friend who had offered my friend a place to stay because they were homeless.

My friend didn't seem hostile due to our adverse past when I drove up, opened the car door, and stepped out. They immediately explained the situation. As a recovering addict, I knew and understood the difficulties we face when attempting to live life on life's terms. Sometimes we fall, sometimes we stand tall. My moments of clean time without rock or alcohol now totaled nineteen years. I was in an excellent place to help my friend reestablish their standing in society, so I agreed to temporarily live with them in the friend's basement until we found something permanent. The offer was a gracious gesture indeed.

Our reunion was joyous; our host fixed dinner to commemorate the occasion, and we all sat around and reminisced. Trey and I continued catching up on our lives in the following days. When we began making plans, at first, we thought about renting an apartment. As fortune would have it, their real estate agent friend offered to assist us in finding a suitable house to buy. This was the perfect solution and something I had always dreamt of doing. My veterans housing benefits guaranteed approval of home loans. Plus, my credit was in good standing.

ONE AFTERNOON, my friend asked if they could use my car to go to the store, to which I consented. Unexpectedly, I did not anticipate this outcome.

They kept my recently purchased used car overnight and returned it early the next day. As we awaited their return home, our host and I discussed our friend's irrational behavior. They asked for my thoughts on the matter, and I didn't hesitate to suggest drugs as an issue. The host's expressionless face and lack of verbal response confirmed my worst conclusion. I learned this was an ongoing problem for them, and the host hoped my presence might help. Despite hearing those words, I could not shake my concern for my car.

As the car pulled into the driveway, its lights flashed by the basement windows. I quickly rushed up the stairs to meet Trey at the side door. Keeping my composure, I walked Trey to the front porch, and we sat. My concern led me to ask what had happened, and they responded honestly. Having experienced similar struggles, I empathized with their situation and offered support.

After our heart-to-heart conversation, we talked about finding a place to live, and my friend began searching for a job. We approached everything with vigilance, and Trey took the lead in handling most of the tasks. They did an excellent job of communicating with their friend, the real estate agent. Everything was going smoothly, and the agent even sent pictures of houses for us to consider, which made me feel excited and anxious at the same time.

I wanted to buy a brick house. When I informed the agent, she sent two more pictures, and one captured my interest. This three-bedroom, two-story brick home with a finished attic and basement was on a quiet residential street on the city's west side. One might hear many stories about that side of town, and many more stories are in the making. This house was, however, not in a neighborhood that was within the area of the plight.

My heart quickened with excitement as I eagerly anticipated the day of our viewing appointment. Finally, another of my cherished dreams was on the brink of becoming a reality. We embarked on a brief journey to meet the agent at the property. The yard was a perfect size, with meticulously trimmed bushes across the front of the house. To top it off, there was even a garage.

The agent explained that the previous owner had installed the iron grates on the doors and windows as an extra security precaution, which added to the house's value.

Upon stepping inside the home, I felt confident, proving this would be the perfect choice. They must have built it specifically for a small family or a couple, and I could feel its untapped potential as we walked through. When the tour concluded, I swiftly agreed to proceed with the purchase with excited enthusiasm.

Accommodations

What words can capture the emotions that surged through me when the agent placed the keys to my new home in my hands? But during the signing process, a sense of dread coursed through my body as I envisioned my friend's name being associated with the mortgage. Backed by a loan from the Veterans Administration, this was my house, and it only made sense for me to be the sole owner.

They didn't mention the issue during the process, choosing to remain silent. And I wasn't going to bring it up. Perhaps they felt it was not their place to inquire about my financial business dealings, but everything turned out fine; it wasn't even mentioned.

Rather than buying a house elsewhere, I had wanted it to be in my hometown. My plan to set down roots and stay there until the end of my days was coming true.

The first order of business was setting up the basement as a shop for Trey to reestablish their tailoring hobby. The furnished attic was perfect for setting up a home office for myself. At the top of the stairs was a closet to the left, and to the right was a short hallway leading to the third bedroom, which would be the office. After purchasing furniture, a fifty-five-inch flat-screen television, and appliances, we moved in. It felt like we were stepping into a dream. My wish had come true, my hope was granted, my yearning was quenched, and my prayer was answered.

I had become a homeowner!

AFTER A SHORT WHILE of living in our new home, my friend received a call informing them that their job application had been approved. The employer wanted my friend to come in and start work at the beginning of the following week. Since I had transportation, it was my obligation to ensure they got to work on time. If they received a paycheck to help with the house responsibilities, driving them to work was mutually beneficial.

Our relationship blossomed over several months spent together in our new home. We began discussing changes or improvements we might make to the house. First, we removed the iron grates from the front living room and bedroom windows to improve the view from the inside. Trey suggested knocking down the wall between the two small bedrooms to create a more oversized, uncrowded main room, and after some thought, I agreed.

After they presented their prior experiences as evidence of their renovation abilities, I placed my trust in their capacity to deliver results. As the project commenced, they unexpectedly encountered an issue pertaining to support beams. They sought advice from a friend and successfully completed the project. However, the removal of two small bedrooms decreased the property value.

To address this, I researched online and found a contractor to extend the house by building a sunroom. The sun deck was added to the back, with a sliding door to the main bedroom. It was a marvelous addition that we hoped would increase the property's value. We invited guests over for a cozy gathering in the new sunporch one evening, where we enjoyed some leisure time among friends.

Becoming Together

I was introduced to Trey's acquaintances right away, and they even took me to the church they had been attending every Sunday. It was a sparsely mixed congregation with a kind, compassionate pastor. The beard he wore made him the perfect candidate for a picture postcard of a grandpa posing with his grandkids. All the church congregation welcomed me openly; I could not sense any malice, ill-will, or dislike among them.

One individual held a significant role in my friend's life, like a costarring character in a movie or play. They worked with several organizations throughout the city and were well-known by many. Knowing my background in the computer field, Trey enlisted me to work with the costar on a project and possibly on more if things worked out. To be regarded with such trust and respect was humbling and an honor I cannot express.

The event organizer, the enigmatic costar, hosted a delightful cookout dinner the night before the big day to set the celebratory mood. A modest crowd gathered, eagerly anticipating the upcoming festivities. What was exciting about this parade was that it would conclude at a park near the city's downtown area. Numerous local vendors would be present, showcasing their distinctive products, and a program with exceptional speakers was scheduled.

Being a part of something that held immense importance to many people was a gratifying opportunity. Knowing that my contributions played a role in the project's success filled me with a sense of pride and joy. Trey shared the same enthusiasm in this endeavor, and it manifested in other areas of their life. Our mutual support for each other strengthened significantly, and we actively participated in various community activities and events. We worked together flawlessly and showed unwavering dedication to each other on personal, professional, and social fronts.

What could go wrong with a seemingly perfect coupling? Several months after the festivities, only slight hints that something wasn't right began to emerge, but I didn't consider them worth mentioning, hoping things would work out. I did not mention something else: the costar came on to me, and they kept doing it repeatedly, but

I maintained the resolve to honor my arrangement until one day, I didn't. But that was later on.

One night, Trey surprised me during one conversation by popping the question. This time, it was about marriage. They asked me to marry them. All positive aspects considered, we made the perfect couple, and they wanted to let the world know of our commitment. Even with the slight reservations in my mind about their occasional slips and their questionable friends trying to get with me, I decided to take the chance, hoping it would encourage them to put forth more effort to stay clean. It could also be a deterrent to their friends' continued attempts.

AFTER WE SPOKE with the pastor, preparations began for the first unconventional wedding to be performed at the church after the Supreme Court ruling granted same-gender unions in 2015.

We married on January 17, 2016, one day after their birthday. It was a day I will never forget. We stood before the pastor and spoke our vows, looking into each other's faces earnestly and reverently. Or at least I thought so. We went on to have our reception and returned to our home as a legally married couple.

Upon initial observation, this arrangement seemed ideal. However, around four months later, following our commitment ceremony, my now lifelong partner began displaying prolonged, concerning behavior. They stayed out until the late hours of the night, not calling or answering calls made to them. It made me sick with worry and filled me with anger and envy. I was outraged because they failed to keep their promise and lacked the decency to at least call and lie so I would know if they were still alive.

My serene composure unraveled beneath the relentless pressure, as well as my partner's intolerable behavior and covert activities. What initially started as a once-or-twice-a-week occurrence spiraled into three or four prolonged, stress-laden nights a week. Despite my determination to maintain sobriety, the frustration and irritability I felt when around them tested the limits of my willpower. As a result, my escalating stress and anger prompted an increase in my marijuana consumption in an attempt to cope with their actions.

After a while, their behavior escalated to the point where Trey started bringing the rock into the house. They locked themselves in the bathroom, turned on the faucet to mask the sound, and indulged in their habit. Each time I heard the water running, I couldn't help but wonder, *What are they doing in there?* The answer became painfully clear one evening when I confronted them at the bathroom door after they had finished their ritual.

It was as I suspected, and my anger resurfaced again. It was increasingly evident that this individual was spiraling out of control, and their relentless addiction was straining our relationship. Equally, our bitterness was noticeable when working on the community activities. Everyone expressed concern.

My partner started falsely accusing me of promiscuous behavior with some of the friends they introduced me to. How foolish would that be? It was all a deflection from their street activities. I found it perplexing because they knew my history of drug addiction. Did they not consider that I would see through the lies and deceptions?

The level of dysfunction within our household rapidly

escalated, turning it into a constant battleground where daily conflicts arose over seemingly trivial matters. These disputes grew so intense that they frequently ended in dramatic exits or verbal confrontations filled with deceitfulness and falsehoods. The unending quarreling placed a heavy emotional and mental burden on me, and it became increasingly evident that my resilience was under strain. During this turmoil, my anger became an overwhelming force, overshadowing my ability to think rationally and rendering the once-comforting marijuana ineffective as a coping mechanism.

Because of that, my mind raced with various thoughts. *What if I were to indulge in their activities with them? Maybe a few instances of them witnessing me partake in their vice and my behavior while under the influence would be a powerful wake-up call, compelling them to reconsider their actions. How would they react? Would they feel responsible for my relapse? If so, would they then quit, and could we stop together?*

Instinctively accustomed to their every move, I intercepted them one day just as they were about to exit the house.

I inquired, "What's up, Trey?"

They responded, and without hesitation, I retrieved the money from my pocket for them to make the purchase. My fallback was my extensive history of sobriety. I believed I could quit whenever I chose. For the sake of our marriage, I was willing to take the gamble.

When they returned, we sat side by side, and nineteen years of sobriety dissolved in a haze of smoke that persisted throughout the night and into the following day.

When the time came to obtain more, waiting for their return tested my patience. I didn't know their whereabouts; it filled my mind with anticipation and speculation. They held the power to dictate how and when I could smoke by keeping their sources a secret, even though I usually had the funds. My partner occasionally left on foot or made calls for a delivery, and it became clear that they had connections with multiple dealers. However, my meeting with any of them was off the table.

One person, on the other hand, started to stand out; they even acquired a nickname, and it was clear that a bond had formed between them and my partner. Listening to their conversations made me increasingly interested in this unknown participant with every spoken word between them. As my partner stepped in and out of their car, I would peek out the window, hoping to glimpse this person. But my efforts were to no avail. Another thing that caught my attention was that this dealer's mode of transportation, always an SUV, changed every three months.

OUR RELATIONSHIP DYNAMICS adjusted slightly when I purchased a gray Chevrolet Malibu, which drove like a dream. It also caught the attention of my partner's friends, who showed a renewed interest in me. Regardless of their stealthy advances, I remained firm in denying their overtures. One day, my partner suggested I drive us to get what we needed. So I started chauffeuring to make the purchases.

During one of our trips, we were supposed to meet the SUV at a specific location. When we reached the spot, we stopped and waited for them to arrive. After a short while, the lights of an approaching vehicle began flashing on and off, signaling us to proceed. We assumed it was the dealer, and I moved forward. As we drew nearer, the driver's appearance caught my attention, sparking a flurry of unexpected thoughts. Yet, voicing any of those thoughts to my partner would have been unwise at that moment, hinting at a potential closeness between the driver and my partner.

At first, sharing with my partner and participating in the activities together seemed like a rousing experience. However, as time progressed, it began to feel monotonous and detached. Furthermore, there were times when my partner would leave and spend the entire night indulging in their habit with someone else instead of being with me. That did afford me the opportunity to seek out other people to smoke with, like that one time with the costar. Or I just smoked by myself.

Driving my partner to work every day had become an unpleasant experience. During the ride, we either sat in silence or argued.

We discussed the situation and agreed it was time for them to buy themselves a vehicle. When we arrived at the dealership, the sales associate presented several options, and we started browsing the available cars. Although my partner initially had reservations about the car that fit their budget, they eventually agreed to purchase it. The only catch was that I had to cosign the loan.

Now that they had a car, trying to reason with them was useless, as we continued to indulge in our vice together, and they embraced their newfound freedom to pursue their desires without any limits. On one rare occasion, when we were at home together, an intense argument erupted that eventually turned into a physical fight. I found myself pinned to the floor near the front door, with them holding me down. Despite the difference in our height and weight, I tried with all my might to break free, but my efforts were in vain.

Realizing I couldn't escape by force, a thought struck me: *What if I lie here, motionless and silent? Perhaps they will interpret this as a form of submission.* That was the plan for getting them off me because I was physically outmatched. After I lay limp, with my mouth shut, they slowly released their knees from my arms, rolled over, and let me get up.

I moved slowly, to avoid causing them to react. After I stood up, we started talking, and I slowly walked toward the kitchen. They stood at the kitchen door, watching me as I walked past them. I walked to the drawer by the kitchen sink, opened it, and politely removed the butcher knife.

Still standing in the doorway between the living room and kitchen, Trey asked, "What are you going to do with that?"

My answer was to lunge in their direction with the knife raised in the air. They ran through the living room and across the small hallway to the main bedroom, with me close behind. Somehow, they found their way to the sunroom with me in close pursuit. They tried to open the door to the backyard, but it was locked. That's when I cornered them. With their hands in the air and chest exposed, it would have taken just a downward thrust, and all the drama and troubles would have ceased.

But I hesitated at the last moment, the knife hovering over their chest. A wave of clarity and fear of the consequences paralyzed my arm.

I couldn't do it. I couldn't kill them.

I lowered the knife and allowed them to move past me. Trey ran, grabbed their phone, and dialed 911.

The police arrived in no time. I barely had a chance to

toss the knife up the stairs, hoping they wouldn't search there.

My troubled friend opened the door for them while I stood in the hall near the staircase. He told them I had pursued him throughout the house with a knife, eventually throwing it up the stairs before they came. All the furniture lay in disarray, and my fifty-five-inch television had suffered the consequences, toppling during the altercation. Fueled by rage, I had impulsively seized the television and yanked it down while in pursuit. In that heated moment, I had intended to use it as an obstacle, hoping to impede their escape. Still, the outcome was far from what I had anticipated. The screen had sustained irreparable damage.

My significant other's derogatory demeanor, promiscuous behavior, and unfounded accusations had laid the foundation for this outrageous situation.

One of the officers found the knife on the stairs and informed the other officer of the discovery. As the cold steel restraints clicked around my wrists, I felt a familiar surge of anger. Much like my previous encounter with law enforcement, being manacled made me angry and left me with a sense of powerlessness and entrapment. They eventually stood me up, recited my rights, and formally imposed domestic violence charges against me.

Riding in the back of a police van was equally appalling due to the cold, hard seats and the echoing noise caused by the steel buckles on the loosened restraint straps clanging against the metal interior of the vehicle. Not knowing what would come next also stirred feelings of dread and anxiousness. *What penalties will be imposed for this charge?* I wondered. My emotions simmered with intense anger during the ride, but it wasn't just because of this situation.

Upon arrival at the police station, I was booked into custody, and my second formal stay behind bars began.

This addiction had dragged me into a vicious cycle once again. Freedom had been taken due to the foolish thought that I could start smoking again with the unrealistic expectation that I could quit and that my partner would change their ways. Also troubling were the days, weeks, and months of relentless cravings to smoke and smoke and smoke. The thought of quitting never crossed my mind.

What might be happening in my house while I was locked up was equally, if not more, concerning. I shuddered to think about it, but down inside, I knew.

Devising Retribution

Upon the arrival of my anticipated release date, a severe constraint was imposed upon me. In the event of an arrest for domestic violence, an automatic ban—a civil protection order—is implemented, restraining the accused party from approaching within twenty feet of the plaintiff and their possessions. Following this, a future hearing is arranged. If the conflicting parties have managed to reconcile their differences, the defendant will be granted permission to regain access to the dwelling. This situation presented a profound predicament, as I lacked any alternative place to stay.

My previous infrequent, methodical solo trips to buy and smoke with others had allowed me to make a few acquaintances. I quickly reached for my phone and stepped out the door of the police station to make several calls, hoping to contact someone who could help. The anxiety and worry lessened when a friend of a friend extended their kindness, allowing me to stay with them until the date of the hearing. Their location was ten blocks from my house, making it tempting to drive by to see what was happening. However, considering the inevitable consequences, delving into an undercover operation to discover drugs and other activities at my house hardly seemed worth the risk.

SOME PEOPLE in the same-gender community may occasionally have ulterior motives for allowing strangers to stay in their homes. While staying with the friend of the friend, I mostly kept to myself, watching television because my host had no computer. The apartment was cozy and spotlessly clean, so it was easy to help with chores. My host also periodically smoked rock, and although we smoked together and shared in the expression once, I did so against my better judgment.

One evening, after a busy day, we decided to relax by watching television and sharing a smoke. My host called the supplier, who promised to arrive in about fifteen minutes. We waited anxiously, hoping they would be on time. The minutes seemed like hours. As the deadline approached, we heard footsteps in the stairwell, growing louder as they neared our door. We glanced at each other across the room with looks of anticipation; we knew whose footsteps they were.

The distinct knocking on the door signaled the dealer's arrival. Standing near the back door after leaving the bathroom, my host directed me to open the door this time. When it opened, a pleasant personality and face with a big smile greeted me. This dealer was new to me; their appearance awakened my attraction instantly. "What is your name?" I asked as they walked by. "You can call me Link," the dealer replied, approaching my host to complete the exchange. When their business concluded, I walked Link back to the door to let them out. We began conversing, which extended to outside, where we casually walked to their ride.

During one of their subsequent visits, we engaged in another in-depth conversation. They made it easy to share, listening closely to every word, and kindly offered to help me however they could. In return, I offered my services as their chauffeur to pick up and deliver their product. We agreed, and I started my new job within a few days. The transportation they had been utilizing was mechanically unfit and visually unappealing. I think it was my car that sealed the deal.

After going on a few solo trips, we began to include two of Links's friends who wanted to join us. The four of us became close and started to hang out together, riding and smoking throughout the day. We eventually earned the nickname "the crew." We began our deliveries in the late morning and continued until the early hours of the next day. When we traveled, we smoked from one delivery spot to another. Sometimes, I even smoked while driving the car.

Once, someone asked me if smoking while driving affected my attention, to which I confidently replied, "No." I have always been a careful driver and have never been involved in an accident, whether under the influence of any substance or completely sober. However, smoking while driving can be dangerous, and other distractions associated with smoking, drinking, and driving could threaten the lives of everyone in the car. Thankfully, such a fate was not ours to encounter.

～

OUR DAILY TRAVELS took us through various neighborhoods, many of which I had never visited. This distinctive opportunity to drive around my birthplace opened my eyes to more of my city's charm and beauty. And meeting new people also proved valuable. But, above all, unrestricted access to rock was the primary benefit. When delivering, we usually stayed in the car and smoked while the supplier walked inside to do business. Occasionally, if the stop was extended, we were invited to go in and smoke.

Upon arriving at a residence, Link would settle into a comfortable spot on either a couch or a chair, placing their cell phone on a table before turning on some classic blues tunes. Despite being young, Link had a deep love for blues music, earning them the nickname "Old School." They didn't indulge in smoking rock, preferring marijuana blunts instead. When the rest of the crew, along with the hosts and myself, gathered to smoke rock, the dealer would often share their blunt with us. Occasionally, the hosts would offer a complimentary drink of alcohol to enhance the celebratory mood of the gathering.

Each morning, I woke to the same routine. The day ahead would be like the day before and the day before that. I picked Link up, smoked my down payment, then picked up the rest of the crew, and we three started smoking immediately. We then drove around the city, delivering to those who had contacted the dealer first and then to the rest. Despite the monotony of our routine, the job was highly lucrative; it was a way for me to get high every day while doing what I loved. Additionally, it was the first and primary phase of my plan of retribution. I was biding my time, setting up scenarios, and waiting for the eventual encounter.

Contemptuous Connotations

I vividly remember the hearing as if the scene were permanently etched in my mind. The judge's bench, made of high-gloss blond wood, sat high off the floor, and the room's trim was adorned with the same material. During the proceedings, the judge asked questions, to which I provided the expected answers. To my surprise, when the same questions were asked of my partner, they also spoke of reconciliation, expressing that we were both willing to continue working out our differences together.

I was not sure that I had made a good impression, and a slight nervousness in my stomach increased as the judge began to render the verdict.

Yes! My performance had been exceptional, and my composure had held up well when I looked at Trey with ill will and anger still fueling my thoughts of vengeance. The charge was closed, and I was allowed to move back into my house.

Now the question was, What will I find when I return?

After my incarceration, I'd bought most of the personal belongings I had with me, so I didn't have much to take home. Neither of us smiled when the door opened, but we greeted each other cordially. It felt good to be home, and to my surprise, the house hadn't been destroyed as I had anticipated. The only urgent matter was to purchase another television. This time, it would be a sixty-five-inch flat-screen. Maybe that's one reason my partner wanted to work it out between us—they couldn't purchase one on their own.

I managed to keep calm and maintain a reasonable attitude with my partner for a few days. All was well until I started leaving the house in the early afternoon and coming back the next morning. Trey started questioning me about where I was going and who I was with as if they were scrutinizing my every move, just like they had me wondering about them when they left the house to purchase the rock and stayed out all night.

One afternoon, Trey entered the front door and introduced a friend to me, explaining that they had dropped by for a haircut. The individual had the appearance of someone less fortunate. It wasn't my place to speak; I remained quiet as they passed me and went to the basement. The "haircut routine" had become a running joke, as everyone knew about my partner's tendency to offer impromptu haircuts to those who piqued their interest. Several of their friends often came by to receive their particular services.

I continued watching television, leaving them to their salon session. Approximately fifteen minutes later, when I strolled into the kitchen, I observed my partner ascending the basement stairs. Their demeanor indicated they had undergone a transformative experience, having relaxed by expressing themselves freely. After a brief verbal altercation, I left the house abruptly, not wanting to see or be around them. Nevertheless, that indicated the possible activities that might have occurred in my house during my absence.

MAINTAINING a straight face as my partner continued to ask me about my friends was challenging. Yet I looked them directly into their eyes and, with a face devoid of emotion, said, "I'm just with friends."

Remember, the only friends of mine they knew of had been Trey's before, so they rightfully asked, "What friends?" as I rushed out the door. Eventually, their curiosity reached another level, and they put two and two together, demanding that when I came in, I bring some rock for them to smoke. This development had yet to be figured into my plan; it would require sharing my compensation.

After one long and exhausting day, I arrived home and decided to back my car into my garage. I carefully maneuvered my car into position and began to turn off the engine when Trey burst out of the house, ran to the garage, and quickly closed the garage door. They started pounding hard on the driver's window with a shovel, looking frantic and yelling for me to hand over the rock. Caution warned me not to open the door.

I repeatedly told Trey I didn't have the rock, but they did not believe me. They became more belligerent and even lay on the hood of my car, demanding that I hand it over immediately. Despite my constant denials, Trey persisted and even stood on the hood of my car and attempted to jump on it. In a desperate attempt to get them off my car, I shifted into drive and accidentally caused a dent in the garage door when it rolled forward. After questioning me three more times, and my repeated responses, my partner finally relented and gave up.

One crucial aspect of my driving duties was ensuring I consistently had a sufficient amount of the rock after my shift ended. Sometimes, but not often, when I returned with little or nothing, like on that day, it caused a verbal altercation. I was accused of lying when I explained why. My partner would say, "You're riding with 'the man'; I know you can do better than that."

The pressure and demands to reveal my friends increased daily, wearing me down. Their insistence came close to becoming physical, and they would lunge toward me while demanding to meet my associates. After extensive deliberation, I decided to throw a bone and disclosed the dealer's nickname. "The person I'm driving is called Link," I said. "Do you know them?" I asked, to which they answered, "No."

Preventing my partner from meeting my friends was gratifying; they were getting a taste of their own medicine—experiencing what it's like to have a partner with hidden objectives. In time, the inevitable meeting between my partner and my friends would occur. Link, who was now essentially my boss, and the other crew members were also curious about the individual I had spoken of with such contempt.

One evening, during our casual gathering, the conversation revolved around my partner's actions, behavior, treatment of me, and overall conduct. Link displayed a clear expression of disgust, another member expressed annoyance, and the other just turned their head.

The introductions would have to occur when Trey returned home from work, which required adding a stop to our route. It would be interesting to see everyone's faces when they finally met. Everyone had been briefed on my partner's tendencies. I anticipated overtures to be directed at someone in the crew, and I expected them to be rejected. Now that we were all on the same page, it was time to initiate phase two.

Assumption of Guilt

As we pulled into the driveway behind my partner's car, I noticed the subdued conversations in mine. When we exited the car, everyone's demeanor changed to cheerfulness as we approached the front door. I welcomed them to my home as we walked inside, and I introduced them to my partner, who immediately met us at the door when it opened. After the introductions, we all sat on the couch, and the boss pulled out the phone to play some blues music, as usual.

Before the event, while driving around delivering, I had limited my substance intake to keep my instincts and senses sharp. The atmosphere was festive, and the boss had brought all the amenities to present a big-time impression. As the evening progressed, everyone seemed in a pleasant mood, roaming freely, laughing, chatting, smoking, and drinking. At one point, Link and I stood in the kitchen discussing what they thought of my partner.

Link believed my accounts concerning my partner's indiscretions, so we devised a plan to reveal and exploit my partner's actual intentions when smoking rock. We called my partner into the kitchen to see which of the two crew members they were attracted to.

"I want the skinny one," Trey answered without delay.

As if that was my cue to deliver my line in a play, I said, "They're mine. You can't have them."

The three of us froze in a still moment of disbelief; neither one had expected me to say that. Nevertheless, I had made it clear that these were my people, and they would not be manipulated.

My partner's willingness to pick someone out of my friends to be with while standing in my presence was the proof I needed. They put on a good front for the others when we left the kitchen, but their resentment couldn't hide from me. I heard it in their voice, and their chipper attitude slowly balanced out. That, however, did not signify that my partner had given up on getting with one of the crew. From that moment, they gave more attention to the other one until our meeting ended. As we walked out the door, I walked between the two to ensure no contact was made.

As PART of our daily routine, we often took a break to relax when I needed a rest from driving. One spot we frequented was well-known by other addicts and dealers, and it was often busy with activity. The person's apartment we frequented was close to my house, just across the main street and four neighborhoods away. Sometimes, while entering and leaving the apartment, I looked around to ensure my partner had not found me.

Our physically challenged host was often confined to home due to limited mobility. Initially, we didn't establish a strong connection. However, after several visits, we gradually developed a mutual understanding and accepted each other without passing judgment. By my observation, it wasn't uncommon for two or four people to be smoking in the apartment upon our arrival. Occasionally, two of them might be engaged in sharing their drug-induced desires in one of the two bedrooms.

I must confess that, after a certain amount of time, I engaged in the latter. However, it's crucial to recognize that in situations where substance, desire, and opportunity exist, there are moments when every person caught in the grip of a rock addiction participates in these forms of self-expression, often regardless of personal inclination. Also ignored was the probability of disease being spread; caution was not of concern. Only the people involved and the settings differed.

We began visiting our designated smoking and distribution spot regularly. As the newcomer and the designated driver, I quickly became a familiar face among the regulars. The atmosphere at times grew festive and crowded, yet surprisingly, no complaints were ever lodged by the neighbors. After several months of frequenting this spot, I learned why the neighborhood tolerated the activity. Whenever my dealer was unavailable, the host would contact other dealers for a delivery. Upon closer observation, this apartment wasn't the only one receiving distributions.

As time passed, my acquaintances and interests grew, and I even became friends with the host. Meanwhile, my partner was still unhappy, constantly insisting that I bring back the crew. I knew exactly what they had in mind. So, one day, we finished our work early, and I dropped off the boss. Then the three of us headed to my house. We had enough rock for everyone to be satisfied. The question was what my partner would do when presented with the opportunity.

Long story short, we arrived at the house and divided the rock; two of us stayed downstairs, and two went upstairs. Several minutes into our separate engagements, I heard a noise from downstairs. I stopped what I was doing to investigate, and it was just what I expected would happen. The crew member who had turned their head, caught my partner's attention, and stayed downstairs with them had succumbed to my partner's seduction.

In a split second, a surge of anger overtook me. I ran over to Trey with my fists balled, throwing rapid punches mere inches from their head. They stumbled and fell to the floor. I continued with three more, then stopped mid-swing. I couldn't do it. I couldn't beat them in the head. Well aware of my partner's tendency to contact law enforcement, I couldn't afford a charge of assault and battery. Plus, the witness in the room could corroborate the story.

I stepped back and looked at their defeated posture. Then disgust replaced rage as I turned and rushed out of the room. Everyone hurried and finished smoking what they had left, and when done, I took the crew members home.

The ride was intense, as my attitude toward that member was not favorable. The trust between us had failed. That wasn't supposed to happen. On the other hand, the skinny member held firm to our commitment, and I was pleased to acknowledge them as my exclusive friend.

In the days that followed, my relationship with the betraying crew member, once amicable, began to fray due to the breach of trust and broken confidence. From another aspect, the blatant, audacious act itself cast a spotlight on my partner's clandestine forays when smoking outside the confines of our residence and during my incarceration. With this revelation now in the open, witnessed by one and experienced firsthand by another, it became abundantly clear that Trey was out of control.

Tranquility Shatters

People had begun dressing for the cooler fall temperatures, so the holiday season was rapidly approaching. Nestled among those holidays is a lesser-known special day that starts the season—my birthday. I decided that this year, I would buy myself a present. Fortunately, my credit score remained favorable, and Kia had an exclusive promotion going on at the time. I knew just the car I wanted. The process flowed seamlessly from start to finish, and as I rolled away from the dealership in my brand-new 2017 Kia Forte, it drove like a well-crafted Swiss timepiece. I was fully aware to whom I owed my appreciation.

I wish you could have seen my partner's face and jaw drop when I rolled up. They yelled, "You got a brand-new car?" while standing at the front door.

In most cases, when someone purchases a new car, their friend might run to look at the car and share the exciting moment with them. This was not such an occasion. This acquisition portrayed the image of financial stability and prosperity. Yet I had not anticipated that not everyone would share my joy.

As my associates expressed in conversation, my partner's treatment of and feelings toward me stemmed from somewhere other than the current circumstances. I am acutely aware that one potential reason for their disgust would be, though private, something cancer took away from me. Delving even further, considering what was revealed about Trey's unfortunate life, we determined that they might harbor envy toward me and anger for what happened in our past. It could stem all the way back to my leaving them for the army many years ago. Even with that, I wanted our relationship to work, so I did whatever was necessary to keep the peace.

More times than not, doing whatever was necessary involved occasional sips of alcohol during smoking sessions. Sometimes, during social gatherings, alcohol was available for those who chose to partake. Everyone seemed to drink more as the holidays drew near, but despite that, I tried to limit my consumption until the night of New Year's Eve 2016. Every fiber in my being began tingling, and my feelings warned me of caution when they asked me to go out to the club.

I did not want to go out that night; my desire to stay in was strong. But their persistent pressuring me to go out would not cease. My plan was for everyone to go out, leaving me alone in the quiet, still, safe atmosphere of my home, enjoying the festivities on television like on many New Year's Eves before. After fighting them off for as long as possible, I finally relented to their requests with a slight attitude, then prepared and went out with them.

The club was jumping, packed wall to wall. Music blared from the huge speakers while everyone on the crowded dance floor pulsed to the mesmerizing beat. My attitude hadn't changed, and regardless of all the pretty and happy people throwing caution aside, none of that changed my mind.

I began drinking heavily, trying to induce a festive attitude; consequently, I bypassed the cheerful part and went into a blacked-out state of mind. The midnight hour signaling the new year came and went without my knowledge.

IT MUST HAVE BEEN the anger that gave me moments of clarity when I woke on my couch. At least whoever dumped me back at home left my car and car keys with me.

Wasting no time getting in my car and pulling out of the driveway, I was on my way to settle a score. How dare Trey drop me at home and then return to the party without me? It wasn't difficult to imagine what might be happening, and they would not get away with it.

That's all I remember until I woke up in the hospital bed with a brace around my neck, hooked to machines, and with casts on my left arm and leg.

As the doctor sat next to me, he explained my injuries. I will never forget this discussion. He also held up the X-rays of my neck and began to illustrate. I had suffered a dislocation of the third and fourth vertebrae, and the third sustained a bone fracture and came to rest against the spinal cord. To avoid any further damage, he had operated and, after realigning the bones, secured a small metal plate to keep them in place. He continued to inform me of the other injuries I had sustained, eventually telling me that I had been in a near-fatal automobile accident.

"You should be dead. Or, at the least, paralyzed," the doctor stated after his formalities concluded.

The instant he spoke those words, my thoughts turned to God. Was it God who had filled me with dread before I headed out? If I had listened to my feelings, this wouldn't have happened. *Why am I still alive?* I wondered.

Despite my resentful transgressions being known, and after all I had done, God had spared my life by mere centimeters. If I had died, I would never have known it in my blacked-out state, the thought of which still causes an empty feeling within me.

Several days later, the police visited me to discuss the accident. They asked me if I had been drinking. In a sense, that question was unnecessary because it had been New Year's Eve, and almost everyone had been drinking. Nevertheless, I answered yes and continued explaining the circumstances. They held up photos and a sketch of the location of my accident. A rippling, cold sensation swept through my body when I saw the damage that had been done.

They showed me where, while driving drunk, I lost control on a hill, hit one curb, crossed the street, hit the other, and then came to rest back across the street with the traffic light poll lying on my car.

I had owned my new car for only three months and didn't even get the chance to enjoy it. Now it was a total wreck. Here I was, back in the hospital, suffering the consequences of my careless, unintentional actions. However, my attempted rebuke of my partner had not driven me to act irrationally in a moment of drunken anger. The combination of substances proved to be a severe and lethal cocktail reminiscent of my military days. Yet, unlike before, this time, I did have an accident, and my body had fallen limp at death's door.

Care and Recuperation

One of our mutual friends, named Darren, eagerly volunteered to nurse me back to health when I returned home. This friend and I appreciated our shared personality traits and enjoyed our time together. Two waves of relief rolled through me when I realized that my care wouldn't be left to my partner alone and that I would not have to hire a home health care aide. Let's not forget that everyone else was on their own during my hospitalization.

A slight tension filled the air when my caregiver arrived.

I spent many days confined to my recliner, feeling miserable and grateful. Being unable to care for myself caused misery, and the gratefulness stemmed from having someone who could care for me. The care and attention I received were so exemplary that anyone would notice our mutual attraction. We had, however, not dared express ourselves, not even when the opportunity presented itself. It was this bond and Darren's support that allowed for in-depth conversations concerning my partner's clandestine activities and treatment of me.

Throughout my days, weeks, and months of recovery, tensions among individuals eased as everyone made a valiant effort to create a conducive environment for my healing. Despite the supportive atmosphere, smoking rock was still a part of my recovery routine. Even following a near-fatal car accident, my top priority, aside from healing, was to keep smoking rock, which proved that it had overpowered me again.

Everyone helped me up to see if I could stand and move independently after removing the cast and neck brace. It took a few times with them supporting me, but I eventually began walking around the house alone. After a while, I ventured outside to breathe fresh air and walk around the yard for exercise. I couldn't have received better treatment from my caregiver. However, it is worth noting that it was God who prevented me from entering death's door and healed my injuries completely.

Renewed Obligations

As mentioned earlier, our deliveries took us to almost every neighborhood and housing development in the city. My curiosity became fixed on one particular neighborhood, house, and customer. This customer never came outside to make the exchange, allowing only their hands to pass the side doorframe. What they did reveal was their butter-scotch-cream skin, to which I am attracted. Our deliveries to Butterscotch became inconspicuously more frequent, and they showed more of themselves each time.

We all had gathered at my house one evening, the usual festivities in play, when the boss received a phone call from a customer. It was Butterscotch. They requested a delivery, but we needed transportation. The only car available belonged to my partner, and the boss wanted to make the sale. The boss knew about my curiosity and attraction to Butterscotch and devised a plan for us to be together. He immediately asked my partner to let me use the car to deliver. At first, he said no, but with a little urging and a bit of substance, the no quickly became a yes.

You see, during a previous smoking session with the crew and two others, one participant agitatedly recounted an incident involving my partner, who had coerced them into the act in the back of their car. Looking into the person's face with total disbelief, I quickly realized another piece of evidence had presented itself. When purchasing my partner's car, they had selected a small, compact, box-shaped vehicle with reclining back seats, presumably for additional storage space. That's where my partner's attack took place—in the back of the car that I had cosigned for, and I believed the claim to be valid.

As I found myself behind the wheel of my partner's car, which was really my car, a surreal feeling came over me. It was hard to grasp that I was driving the car in which the attack had taken place. Also astounding was that the boss and I had successfully convinced Trey to relinquish the car. Nevertheless, I was on my way, and what lay ahead would make me forget all about my troubles.

Their house was close to mine, about a four-minute drive at most. When I pulled onto the street, I became anxious about the meeting; finally, I would see all of them, not just their arms and a shoulder.

When I pulled into the driveway, the side door opened immediately, and I could hardly believe what my eyes saw. They seemed anxious for my arrival as well, walking to the car hurriedly and looking closely to ensure that I was the only occupant. When they reached the passenger door, they opened it and got in. We greeted each other, but that was the preliminary of what we both knew was about to happen.

My delivery took longer than expected, and Trey was furious when I returned home so late.

I didn't care. I gave them the keys, spoke to the boss and the crew, and smoked a little more until they went home. My partner had not expected that to happen and didn't know how to deal with it after the fact, faced with the reality that I had taken the car and used it as a lure as they had done many times before.

After completing physical therapy, which gave me a clean bill of health, I urgently needed to purchase another car. I had to act quickly because I no longer had my previous car and had stopped the automatic payments. Since it would take some time before the missed payments showed on my credit report, my credit was still good. In a relatively short time, my search led me to purchase a gray 2014 Cadillac ATS, the same year and color as my previous Malibu. It also made me proud to have finally obtained such a prestigious automobile.

Every crew member was awestruck when I picked each of them up separately. The solemn tone in their voices expressed their struggle to comprehend that they were riding in a Cadillac with a chauffeur at the wheel. The boss had made temporary arrangements for transportation during my unfortunate incident and subsequent recovery but was eager to resume deliveries riding in my new car with me. As was the ritual, they dispensed the rock, and we began smoking immediately.

6

ABSENT HELL'S FLAMES

The Welcome Mat

Link suggested it first. "Let me use your house as my spot to distribute my product, and I'll pay you," they said.

Usually, this statement would prompt a person with a substance use disorder to start negotiating the terms. This was such a time. The proposal required thought because the payment had to be split with my partner. So, after a couple of minutes of reflection and working out the payment amount that we deduced would keep my partner at bay, I agreed to the proposal.

In the days that followed, my partner and I rarely argued as long as rock was available, and everyone behaved well together. That's how it started. We smoked, they drank, and we received periodic visits from customers who came to buy the product. Our home quickly became a hub of activity in our part of town. This interrupted my interest, but it was an opportunity to meet customers firsthand and gain respect as the residence's owner. Each day, we had unique encounters with eager customers, some buying and leaving and others staying to partake in the usual ritual.

My partner began to exhibit suspicious behavior, and the atmosphere varied between involved and calm. Their attitude resurfaced again, and they spewed accusations, projections, and allegations. Their animosity was perplexing and beyond my understanding. Yet, in the interest of honesty, I must admit that by this time, some accusations against me held a degree of truth. Although I had concealed my actions, I took steps to ensure that no one outside our circle knew about them.

This substance-driven activity continued unabated for several months. Instead of us delivering, customers now came to us to purchase their substance. As the days, weeks, and months of substance consumption progressed, so did the selling of the product and the drug-induced acts of desire associated with smoking it. Whether upstairs, down-stairs, or in between, the setting I had allowed to develop was thick with drug deals, debauchery, scandal, and overt, covert, and erotic expression in which a significant number of people entering had participated.

MEANWHILE, along with being hospitalized for an urgent medical condition, our associate in the apartment learned that they had to vacate their residence, adding additional stress to their recovery. In a compassionate gesture, the boss quickly devised a plan. He suggested my house as a place for our associate to stay during their recovery until they found other lodgings. Far be it from me to deny someone shelter in their time of need, especially when it involves medical recuperation.

A feeling of anticipation filled the air when the hospital released the associate, especially since they hadn't smoked in a while. When they sat in the car and closed the door, one crew member handed them the smoking apparatus immediately. We all began smoking as I pulled away from the hospital and headed toward home.

When we arrived at my house and got our associate settled in, we all sat in the living room to smoke and chat with each other. However, Trey, who remained long enough only for the introduction and to collect a payment, swiftly retreated downstairs.

When the meet-and-greet session concluded without one of the leading participants, the boss gave us something for later. My partner, who was already downstairs, missed out. The dynamics in the house changed dramatically with our newly acquired houseguest moving in. My partner's displeasure at my decision to bring someone into the house was evident. They and Willie, our houseguest, barely spoke to or even made eye contact with each other for weeks. The air between my partner and me was thick for days, with an uncomfortable silence—the desired conclusion to phase three.

Beneficial Coincidence

Word spread across the city that my house was now the go-to place, at least on that side of town. Many of those we delivered to kept coming to our door, and a few were new to me. On slow evenings, some regulars would gather in the living room to smoke, talk, and watch television until it was time to leave. My partner was in and out but remained polite for the most part as long as there was substance to smoke. The boss conducted business in the kitchen or sometimes upstairs in my office, and I was compensated generously.

Several individuals stood out from the crowd. One of Willie's friends was very expressive, straightforward, and candid, and they liked to talk a lot. Another person was an acquaintance of the boss's—tall, well-fed, and well-groomed. If you hadn't sat and smoked with them, you couldn't tell from their appearance that they did. They had an unassuming demeanor. "Gentle giant" comes to mind. By now, almost every person coming through our door came because of the boss and, subsequently, me.

The boss's friend stopped by the house periodically to smoke with us but did not participate in any of the self-expression sessions. They gained my respect with how they carried themselves, which was noticeably different from the others. One day, as I, the houseguest, Gentle Giant, and two others sat in the living room chatting, smoking, and laughing, the setting was calm and relaxing.

As the side door opened into view, Trey stepped through. Gentle Giant and I were sitting next to each other, where anyone entering the house through either door could see us. My partner addressed only Gentle Giant, ignoring everyone else in the room. I had already been informed of my partner's attraction to Gentle Giant, who had rejected their advances. The emphasis in my partner's voice indicated their displeasure at seeing Gentle Giant and me sitting next to each other on the couch.

"Get up! I'm tired and want to lay down, and you're sitting on my bed," my partner said, walking to and standing over me.

Everybody knew that they slept in the basement; this

was an attempt to break up the gathering and separate Gentle Giant and me. At one point, my partner called Gentle Giant into the kitchen for a brief conversation. Brief it was, and when they returned to the room, my partner again showed irritation with Gentle Giant, who sat back down next to me.

My partner went away for a while but returned and confronted me again, only in a more agitated mood this time.

"Get up," they said, their voice louder than before.

"No," I said. "I'm with my company, and you know you sleep downstairs."

The next time, Trey demanded I get up, forcefully grabbing my arm and propelling me off the couch and onto the coffee table, which shattered beneath me. My partner lunged at me, attempting to strike me, but I swiftly evaded every blow. I wrestled my way out from under them with all my might and swiftly headed to the kitchen. Unfortunately, as I crossed the doorway, they rushed behind me and forcefully tackled me to the floor again. A fierce struggle followed, but I effectively blocked each swing directed at me. When it seemed like our contest had reached a stalemate, our houseguest loudly implored Gentle Giant to intervene and break up the fight.

Gentle Giant wasted no time coming to my rescue, yanking my partner off me and standing between us as I got off the floor. Anticipating the imminent attack, I had grabbed a broken metal hanger, the only object within reach, and thrust it toward my partner's neck in self-defense.

Willie's outspoken friend had called the police immediately; strangely enough, so did my partner at the same time. It was perplexing. My partner was the attacker, and four others witnessed it. Why would they call 911?

When two police officers arrived, one stayed in the kitchen with my partner and Gentle Giant, and the other came into the living room with the rest of us. When the officer in the living room asked us what had happened, everybody started speaking simultaneously.

I heard parts of what was being said in the kitchen. Trey was lying, and Gentle Giant was pointing it out. I knew I had hit my mark when the officer in the kitchen asked about the blood. One person finally spoke and told the officers that my partner had jumped on me for no apparent reason other than to disrupt our social gathering. The officer asked us if we had been smoking, to which we honestly answered yes. We received a gracious warning as they manacled my partner, who was then charged with domestic violence and escorted out the side door—the desired conclusion to phase four.

Unexpected Expectation

When Trey finally walked out the door, each person in the house breathed a sigh of relief, their tension dissipating with the sound of the door closing. The constant struggle for control, coupled with their attraction toward anyone who caught their eye, had been a continual distraction to deal with. With them gone, the house was finally ours—a sanctuary of peace. The days and nights became calm and manageable as we savored the calming tranquility.

During a conversation with the boss, the crew, and the houseguest, I shared an incident that happened between my partner and me earlier. While on a break from our deliveries, I'd gone home one night to get something. I unlocked the side door, but it wouldn't open. I pushed a couple of times, then realized it was not stuck but secured internally. I had to bust in the side door to enter my house. When I stepped through the door and looked into the living room, what I saw alarmed me.

A naked individual was sitting on my couch. Trey jumped up from the other end, partially clothed. As I walked closer, I saw something on the end table. Upon closer observation, I saw that it was a needle. My partner's surprise, visible anxiety, and disarranged state suggested they had been using drugs and were interrupted. The scene had taken me aback, but I maintained my composure enough to tell the naked person that it was my house and they needed to leave now.

They began to dress hastily and rushed past me out the door. My partner and I exchanged words, and I left and returned to work. I couldn't stand being around or seeing them one moment longer.

That incident had remained in my mind until that day when my partner threw me on the coffee table. Those weren't the actions of a rational person, nor was it usual for them to act in such a manner, even after smoking rock. Everyone who had witnessed the attack knew this to be abnormal behavior for Trey, and my disclosure about this incident revealed the possible cause.

ONE DAY, when Willie and I were alone in the house, I heard a knock at the side door. Willie was in the bedroom, so I got up from the couch to answer it. As I swung the door open, my heart sank to my feet when I saw Trey standing there with a big smile. It had been only two weeks since the altercation and the charge of domestic violence that barred them from coming to the house, yet they were bold enough to show up anyway. I wasted no time slamming the door in their face.

I immediately informed Willie, who relayed the incident to the boss, who couldn't believe it either. Following my partner's arrest for domestic violence, officers advised me to file an extension of the automatic protection order (which I did). They instructed me to call if my partner violated the order, which would lead to potential jail time. Understanding the gravity of the situation, I decided to contact them regarding Trey's brief visit, which thankfully turned out to be the last. However, as I walked out of the corner store on the main street one day, I heard someone call my name. When I looked, it was Trey standing at the corner, straddling a bike.

No, I did not speak. Looking away immediately, I began walking down my street to escape them. Halfway down the street to my house, they flew by me on the bike and yelled, "What's up?" as they passed. My frustration skyrocketed because I knew it would be less concrete to prove this incident compared to the last, so I reluctantly let it go. At least I knew they hadn't put my partner in jail yet.

Either way, after that sighting, I never saw them again.

EVERYTHING WAS everything with my partner gone, and our operation was up and running smoothly. Things ran so smoothly that the boss wanted to experiment, at our urging, of course. They told me not to get credit from anyone else, then entrusted each of us with an amount of rock to sell and told us to return the proceeds when we next got together.

The boss was adjusting the hours spent away from home, which left the rest of the crew to ourselves most days. We still welcomed guests to participate in smoking sessions, though the expression sessions had all but faded away. During one smoking session, the boss couldn't come to the house, and I couldn't leave, so one of the guests called a dealer they knew.

I was sitting on the couch when someone answered the knock at the side door. As soon as the person stepped through the door and turned toward the living room, I recognized them as the person who drove the SUV—that moment was imprinted in my mind forever.

They first said, "I know whose house this is. Trey lives here."

I immediately replied, "It's my house, and they don't live here anymore."

After confirming that the house was mine and my partner was gone, I became curious about this young dealer who knew my partner so well.

I attempted to subtly extract information from the guest who had called them, and I was surprised at their willingness to share specific details. After the dealer walked out the door, I watched out the side window as they climbed into the SUV and drove away. I soon understood, after piecing everything together, the nature of their relationship with my partner. Their comment revealed they had been to my house before, likely during my incarceration. The unsettling implication—that this person, known for their widespread appeal, had taken advantage of my absence—was a thought I chose to ignore.

~

EACH INDIVIDUAL who used my house as a rendezvous point had unique arrangements with their specific distributors. Now that they had begun frequenting my house, it was only fitting that I establish my own arrangements.

Most didn't know about my financial stability. Yet I eagerly divulged the information to receive some rock on credit when money ran short. After a while, I was in debt to four dealers at one point; the boss was one of them. I owed hundreds of dollars at month's end. But every dealer received payment promptly when the date arrived, and I even purchased more during the transaction.

On occasion, remitting payment meant having one of the dealers take me to the bank. On the day the attractive SUV dealer was to be paid, I suggested they take me to the bank to withdraw the funds. That was because I wanted to quell any misgivings about my ability to obtain the funds on my own, return home, and call for them to come.

When I climbed up into the new SUV, the dealer's charisma overwhelmed me. I couldn't help myself, and I spoke of my attraction directly to them.

There was no response—neither a look nor words said. They didn't even acknowledge that I had gotten in the car. They looked straight ahead, put the SUV in reverse, pulled out of the driveway, and proceeded to the bank.

I forget what brought about this comment, but the dealer's later threat about the money during the drive to the bank made me uneasy.

"Don't make me put my hands on you," they said commandingly.

Already agitated with the cold reception, I replied daringly, "You won't put your hands on me."

Only after our exchange did I realize that the dealer had someone on the phone who heard every word. That person asked questions about who was talking. "You going to let them talk to you like that?" they said.

The dealer's responses were stiff with aggression, and I will not repeat what was said. When we reached the bank, I withdrew the funds, left the bank, got in the car, and handed the dealer an envelope with the money.

They had little to say on the return trip; the money spoke louder than my words. Being with them and observing their dismissal of my interest gave me insight into one possible element of my partner's relationship with them. Also, it explained why my partner's portion of the conversations with this dealer were so timid, soft, and unassuming.

Opportunity Presents Itself

One reason for the constant deliveries and people coming to buy from me was that my transportation was no longer operational. Approximately one month after my partner's arrest, I had an accident while driving my Cadillac on one of the main streets. When the RAV4 in front stopped at a stop sign, I looked down at my cell phone for a quick second. I anticipated the RAV4 had moved, but it hadn't. Unconsciously expecting that it had, I began to accelerate and inadvertently rammed into the back of it. The front of my Cadillac crumbled like paper.

Knowing that my financial situation could not withstand automotive repairs, indeed not of that magnitude, I reported it as a total loss. So that began my second extended period without transportation in my adult life. The longest was approximately one year. After a while, not having transportation was not a problem; at least I wasn't driving all over the city all day long. If I had an appointment or needed to shop, I could always call an Uber or a Lyft.

Most evenings, after everyone had left, Willie retreated to the main bedroom, and I walked upstairs to mine. Most times, after a marathon smoking session, we slept for most of the following day. At the time, I had been smoking rock every day for four years, stopping and sleeping only due to exhaustion, hospitalization, or incarceration. My house began showing signs of neglect; the garage door hung broken on its rail, the yard wasn't maintained, and we hadn't put any food in the house since my partner left. We bought food only for ourselves individually.

Over time, I began to regret every wish I had to get high every day. Nothing about it was glamorous in any way. The expressions of desire were passive and empty. The dealers willingly put their customers in debt. And we kept spending money until it was gone but kept on smoking anyway. It wasn't like I didn't know what to do, but I didn't want to leave my house or put it in the hands of others.

In one moment of clarity, while lying on my makeshift bed, I woke up to the feeling of dread. I decided to contact my recovery counselor and friend, Evan, for advice. I explained the situation during the conversation and expressed my reluctance to leave. When I was sharing my plan to make it all stop, Evan expressed that it wouldn't solve the problem. They aptly pointed out that this unconventional approach wouldn't resolve the underlying issue, as my addiction wouldn't be stopped with the removal of others. I will not share their exact response, but I will paraphrase what they said next.

"Forget that house! I'm trying to save your life!" Evan said resolutely.

Yet even those words were not enough to make me walk away.

I came up with a strategy to get rid of all the drug dealers from my home. Whenever two or more dealers were present downstairs, I would call the police from upstairs in my bedroom and alert them to the illicit drug activity happening in my house. The police would then arrive and apprehend everyone except me, since I had made the call from upstairs.

It became apparent that the house had been subject to surveillance for several months, as was confirmed one night.

The police intercepted an individual around the corner from the house and questioned them about where they had come from. The person answered all of their questions truthfully. The police then allowed the person to return to the house, and when they arrived, they were eager to tell us about the police encounter.

We all looked at this individual with disbelief, as if they were entirely unhinged. The mysterious question remained —Why would someone willingly disclose to law enforcement their involvement in illicit activities and divulge the location, thereby jeopardizing everyone else's freedom?

Before and after this startling disclosure, a series of incidents took place with individuals who found themselves detained by the authorities after leaving my house. I wonder why they never raided my house even though they could have done so at any time.

WHEN THE FEELING of dread happened again, it completely overpowered me, prompting me to seek emergency assistance.

When I woke up, I looked around myself and was repulsed by what I saw. Rolling off my mat and struggling to stand, I finally reached for my phone. I called the Veterans Administration Suicide Prevention Hotline. The gentleman who answered was attentive to my situation and stayed on the phone with me until the paramedics arrived. Willie witnessed my departure and informed the boss of the development. The boss wasted no time checking on me and kept activities at my house in order during my hospital stay.

Recalling the details of what happened after leaving the house proves to be difficult at this time. Pretty much everything was a blur from the moment they wheeled me away from the house except the faint memory of my stay in the mental health ward at a local hospital. I do remember them weighing me. I had lost twenty pounds. My memory picks up with a stay in a local nursing home. The official cause of admission was dehydration, probably brought about by my irrepressible substance abuse. Still, I can recall almost nothing of my stay there. But when my care concluded, they released me with a clean bill of health.

Everybody stood outside waiting to greet me when I arrived back home.

"You look terrific! You're glowing," someone said as I walked up to them. That statement made me smile, and it was a pleasure to be home. Unfortunately, everything had stayed the same regarding the availability of the rock. Someone handed me an apparatus and a rock, saying, "I know you're ready after all that time without it." As much as I wished I had taken that opportunity not to start again, I passed up the perfect chance to do so. My addiction was rekindled in less than ten minutes after my return home. The glow faded with each exhale of smoke.

The Inevitable

Continuing from where I had left off, the intensity of my addiction peaked within a matter of days. Link consistently supplied me with rock, often extending credit without me asking.

One morning, a subtle noise aroused me from sleep. As I reluctantly opened my eyes, I witnessed the boss walking away from me. Hindered by my inability to move and barely able to speak, I managed to mumble, "Link!"

The figure continued its sneaky stride toward the stairs. At that moment, with the substance right in front of me, there seemed to be no alternative but to surrender to the temptation and indulge once more.

It was happening all over again, only this time, the boss was leaving it where it would be the first thing I would see when waking. During the day, Willie and I smoked it either together in the living room, separately in our rooms, or together when company came over. Either way, the constant availability of rock and the smoking of hundreds upon hundreds of dollars almost every day for months on end began to affect my senses.

Back when the crew had started coming to my house and we held smoking and desire sessions in my bedroom office, one crew member had carried with them a hidden adversary. Due to that member's physical limitations, I suggested they sit in my recliner. The days following revealed annoyance as something kept jumping on and biting me. At the time, I didn't know what it was or where it came from, but after an exhaustive search, I found where the infestation originated. It was the recliner.

I prepared to dispose of the recliner the following day but couldn't put it on the curb for trash pickup due to the bugs, so I dumped it behind the garage. But even after I removed the recliner, the infestation persisted, making staying in the room and sleeping difficult. Bedbugs not only crawl and bite but also leap onto their unsuspecting victims. They are also attracted to blood, and my bed matting was on the carpeted floor where they had migrated, so I was constantly bitten.

It had gotten so bad that they were between the walls and the carpet, eventually spreading throughout the house and even being carried out on unsuspecting guests. Due to the sensitive nature of our activities, we determined that calling an exterminator was not recommended. We didn't have the money anyway. So the crew got together and purchased the chemical treatment to rid my house of the pests. It goes without saying that my friendship with that crew member became suspect even then.

OFTEN, during the days of consistent smoking, feeling the rock coursing through my veins became slightly alarming. When it first happened, I felt the substance flowing through my spinal cord in the back of my neck. Frozen in disbelief, I allowed it to continue coursing into my brain so I could experience the effect. It immediately produced a sensation of euphoria, then an uncontrollable thirst for more.

The yearning to reach that ecstasy high again is over-powering when the sensation begins to dissipate. During my time riding with the boss, the experience revisited me many more times, as was apparent in my hospitalizations. From day to day, stretching into weeks without interruption, my habit fed on rock constantly.

During a solo smoking session, I began feeling something touching my skin; at least, I thought so. I looked but couldn't see anything. I concluded that the treatment to rid my house of the pests had not worked completely. Buying additional treatments was off the table financially because I was deeply in debt, so I devised a plan. I could light a can of shoe polish on fire, let it burn until it produced enough smoke to fill the room to fumigate it, then extinguish it. I had done it once, right after the first treatment, and I thought it helped.

I placed the shoe polish can in the center atop the space heater, lit it on fire, then hurried downstairs to take one last puff.

When I returned to my bedroom, it seemed warmer than usual when I reached the top of the stairs. As I turned to walk down the short hallway to the room, I saw smoke coming from below the tarp covering the door. When I rushed to the door and quickly pulled the tarp aside, a tower of fire greeted me. It had engulfed the space heater and that section of the sizeable wooden corner desk that my partner had purchased for me.

Without hesitation, I turned and ran to the closet. The first item on the rack near the closet door was my leather coat. I grabbed it and ran back to the fire.

When I snatched the tarp back, I could see that more of the desk had caught fire and was close to burning the ceiling. I used both hands to spread the jacket. I planned to use it to smother the fire, but my effort became precarious when the blaze engulfed the jacket and jumped out a few inches from my face.

Overcome with fear, I turned and ran downstairs to tell Willie that the house was on fire and we had to leave.

They yelled, "Get some water and put it out!"

I, in my panicked state, wasn't thinking. I ran past Willie

and the front door, then went into the kitchen to get water to extinguish the fire, not heeding my own warning to leave.

Water splashed everywhere as I frantically ran through the house. When I reached my room, the tarp showed signs of burning around the edges. Not deterred, I snatched it back, and a thick black-and-gray plume of smoke hit me in my face. The bucket of water fell to the floor; the smoke blinded me instantly, simultaneously entering my nose and mouth and reaching my lungs within seconds.

My body spasmed and cramped into a bent position in response to my lungs' sudden trauma. All I could do was use my memory and hand to navigate back downstairs, away from the inferno. Willie was in the kitchen and already on the phone with 911 when I stumbled into the living room. With what breath I could muster, I yelled to them, "We got to get out!"

"Why did you set the house on fire?" they asked as we finally made it outside. If I could have answered, my response would have been denial because, technically, I didn't set the house on fire.

Concerned about our well-being, some neighbors had gathered outside to observe the event. Willie's questions continued, none of which I answered. When the paramedics and fire trucks arrived, I was still doubled over from the pain in my chest, barely able to see, and continuing to cough up black soot. Finally, someone touched my shoulder and asked if I was alright; my response was another incapacitating cough.

Before the paramedics escorted me to the EMS vehicle, I saw the firefighters carrying the hose inside the house. I was hoping that they had arrived in time to save it.

I asked one of the paramedics, "Are my facial hairs singed?"

She answered, "No," much to my relief.

They helped me into the vehicle and instructed me to lie on the stretcher so they could assess the severity of my smoke inhalation and provide the appropriate treatment.

While I lay there, still unable to breathe three times without coughing, the burning sensation in my lungs became more evident. When I informed the paramedic who helped me, the other one said, "It's not that bad. Stop coughing."

My anger could not break through the pain in my chest and my inability to breathe. Those problems took priority at the time. In addition, responding to the sarcastic comment would have likely caused a scene, and that prompted me to try harder not to react.

As we pulled away from the house, I couldn't help wondering how bad the damage might be. I wondered if it had burned beyond repair or if the firefighters had extinguished the fire in time, preventing it from doing extensive damage.

My thoughts soon returned to my immediate health crisis as we neared the emergency room entrance. When we arrived, medical staff swarmed me, swiftly transferring me to another stretcher and wheeling me into one of the treatment rooms. After quickly moving me to a stationary bed, they immediately began administering treatment. My eyes began to clear after being washed with eye solution made for such instances. People dressed in white came and left, some taking blood samples, others ensuring the oxygen tube was secure on my face with no obstructions. The coughing and chest pain began to ease after they administered the oxygen treatment, and my breathing became clearer as I lay there.

While eating a snack in the hospital bed, I couldn't help

but reflect on the distressing events that had brought me here. It was like a nightmarish movie—my journey of drug addiction spanning multiple states. I had smoked in empty houses, in other people's homes, in my home, in others' cars, in my car, in abandoned cars, in old buildings, and even out in the open; we smoked anywhere that was convenient. Every day was a relentless cycle of smoking sessions. The mix of personalities—some narcissistic—had contributed to a toxic scene. My rock habit had taken over my life again.

Every morning, the ritual of smoking rock had come first before thinking even about breakfast, and that usually meant skipping other meals because that drug subdued any feeling of hunger. Also, making my living situation uncomfortable were the constant visits from familiar and unfamiliar faces coming and going all through the day and night.

During those last tumultuous days, months, and years before the fire, the burden of my existence weighed heavily upon me like a fleece bathrobe soaked in oil. With each passing day, the weight grew heavier, making my desire to break away distressingly inadequate. I prayed many prayers —most times after we had smoked and spent everything— asking for the strength to stop. But neither recovery tools nor my willpower could assist me at that time; only by divine intervention could I break free. So, with all of the humility within me, I prayed and asked God to intercede.

How mysterious are the ways of God? No man knows how God's answers may materialize; one must be rooted in the Holy Spirit to recognize God's response. God knew my plight, my struggle, and the strength of my faith and trust. Could the fire I lit with my hands be God's answer to my prayer?

Someone recently asked me if God answered my prayers, to which I replied, "Yes, all of them."

"Not all of them!" they exclaimed.

"All of them," I said. Even the prayers I shouldn't have spoken. That's how I relearned to pray with conviction."

So, my mouth has spoken of remorse and a request for serenity and stability. Could the fire have answered my prayer?

7

REDEMPTIVE RESOLUTION

Transitionally Advantageous

There's a term some use when a decision is either evident or the only choice that makes sense. My choice not to return to my house was, as they say, a no-brainer. That was my out, my escape. In the moments of my most profound desperation, it is my deep belief that God used my hands to answer my prayers.

Realizing this while lying in the hospital bed, I felt a gratifying sense of ease come over me. In due time, my health improved to the point where the doctors recommended my discharge, but I didn't have anywhere to go. However, there was my recovery counselor, who would answer my call and assist me upon my release.

My counselor quickly responded with good news. A friend owned Victory House, one of several homes used as nonprofit transitional housing for honorably discharged veterans. After briefing their friend about my situation, I was allowed to move in. Being away from those people and my house was technically the beginning of another aspect of recovery. When given a harmonious space to rest and rejuvenate in, the mind begins to unravel and discard the negative nuances and replace them with new activities and memories.

When I stepped through the door of the transitional house, the first thing that caught my eye was the floor, which was polished to a high-gloss shine. Everything in the house was immaculate; there was no dust or dirt anywhere. The two current residents welcomed me, and one made an extra effort to ensure I felt at home. Being in a house that clean made me wonder who handled the upkeep. Of course, the residents kept the place clean, and their efforts were evident based on the appearance. The maintenance would also become a part of my responsibilities, which wouldn't be challenging. The only requirements for room, board, and meals were making an affordable monthly payment and keeping the common areas and our personal spaces clean.

When the hospital staff returned my clothes, they smelled of smoke from the faint hint of soot embedded in the fabric, so I had to throw them away. The establishment proprietor graciously purchased several clothing items for me, necessities for someone who had nothing. At the house, the resident who was attentive to my needs, supplied me with jackets and coats in preparation for the winter months that would soon greet us. For their compassion, I will be forever grateful, but the benefits didn't stop there. The proprietor had also created a supportive activity program aimed at helping veterans maintain sobriety and transition into civilian life.

~

DEVELOPING A ROUTINE WASN'T DIFFICULT; only three of us were in the house, and we mostly stayed to ourselves in our bedrooms. Sometimes, even though we all had televisions in our rooms, one of us might relax and watch the flat screen in the living room. We ate breakfast and lunch when we wanted, and a caterer brought dinner daily. The proprietor had established a weekly twelve-step recovery meeting, which was held downstairs in the furnished basement, and held other activities outside, like gardening and woodworking. On holidays, they had special gatherings for the veterans and their families.

Being there felt like a divine intervention had occurred—like God's hand had descended, firmly grasped me, forcefully pulled me out of hell, and placed me in a realm of serenity. The atmosphere and surroundings emanated a profound sense of peace and tranquility; however, an unexpected and disheartening occurrence took place not long after my arrival. Even in the most seemingly idyllic circumstances where drugs are prohibited, they infiltrated this haven of healing anyway.

The hour was late, around ten thirty or eleven p.m., when I heard a faint tapping sound. Grabbing the television remote to turn the volume down, I lay still and quiet in an attempt to pinpoint where in the house the sound came from. After hearing the curious noise randomly in different areas of the home on different days for weeks, I asked the other resident one morning at breakfast, "Did you hear that tapping last night?" Along with confirming that they had, they told me the cause. Our attentive housemate was crushing up pills and then sniffing the powder to get high.

I was infuriated. Not two months into my new life in a supposed drug-free environment, and someone was getting high right under my nose.

No, that wasn't a pun.

I should have known, but I immediately called the proprietor, who handled the situation swiftly and without incident. The tapping never happened again. However, it seemed as if having quelled one intrusion into my attempt to rejuvenate, another presented itself. The resident who informed me about the tapping had a pleasant demeanor, but their energy level was off the charts. They always had remarks to make, stories to tell, and idle chatter to draw attention to themselves.

At the time, I smoked cigarillos and often left the house to sit in the backyard to take a smoke break. Chatterbox often left me alone but sometimes wanted to talk, so they came outside to find me. I did whatever I had to do to keep the conversation short. I'd walk around and look at the plants in the garden or walk to the front to sit on the porch to watch the traffic go by—whatever it took to get them to leave me alone. They finally got the hint, as was evident in their conversations, which became shorter, more substantive, and void of negativity.

DURING MY SEVEN-MONTH stay at Victory House, my top priority was recovering and staying away from the rock at all costs. It was too soon for me to return to that side of town to check on my house. I didn't know what I would find, and I was worried that one of the dealers I still owed money to might see me. To my astonishment, while I was staying at Victory House, one of the three who were looking for me found me—the boss.

The house dynamics had changed; Crusher and Chatterbox had moved out, and a new resident had moved in.

One day, someone knocked at the front door, and the new resident, whose room was at the front of the house, left their room to answer. From up in my room, I heard the faint sound of a female voice speaking, but I couldn't make out her words. Suddenly, the new resident called me downstairs to the door because the woman had asked if I lived there.

Who could this person be who's asking for me? I wondered.

When I reached the door and looked outside on the porch, I saw the female, but I didn't know her. She asked me if I knew someone whose name I didn't recognize. I replied, "No."

Then she mumbled something as she turned away, preparing to step off the porch. When I turned and looked at the car at the curb, somebody was waving at me from it, which caught me off guard.

"Is that Link," I asked, to which she answered yes.

It was the boss! *How did they get my address?* I wondered. Imagine the top of your head turning molten red with anger. That's precisely how it felt to see the boss at my sanctuary. But somehow, I managed to maintain my composure and cautiously strolled toward the car with a smile, not knowing what to expect as the space between us shortened.

The young lady got in the car, and Link proceeded to hold a conversation with me that was initially supportive of my sobriety. But it eventually turned to the money owed.

When a person with an addiction owes a dealer money, that dealer remembers how much is owed, down to the last cent; if they paid on time or late; and how many days late the payment is. Some dealers let us pay late only once or twice, and then they might hurl threats to get us to start paying on time. After all that time, Link remembered the exact amount I owed, even offering me a discount for good measure.

"You owe me this amount, but I'll take off this much. Then you can give me a part of the balance now and pay down on the rest a little at a time," Link proposed.

With the sound of their last word, I instantly knew this was a ploy to get me hooked again. That rage swelled up inside me instantaneously. *How dare this individual come here, congratulate me on stopping, but attempt to coax me back into the darkness in the same breath*, I thought. Only evil would be so bold and cavalier.

I turned my head away in disbelief, and I had to gather my thoughts to formulate the appropriate response.

"At the end of next month, and I'll pay all of it" was the only viable conclusion. Our conversation turned to idle chatter; we even discussed the new car and the new girl-friend. When the pleasantries terminated, Link slowly pulled away, and I stormed back into the house with a severe attitude.

My fellow resident noticed my agitation and inquired about the cause. When I explained, they understood and promised to be more vigilant. My anger and the unsettled feeling in my chest and stomach prompted me to inform the proprietor of the incident.

What the proprietor said after I explained what happened shocked me into a sense of empowerment.

"You're not giving them any more money," they said. "You've given them enough money already."

Instantly, with those words, the financial burden of owing three dealers all of that money vanished.

There was just one other matter of concern. Now that Link had found me, it would only be a matter of time before the others did. As it turned out, my move-out day was the following weekend. The proprietor owned several residential properties, and one was an apartment building. There was a vacant apartment available, so instead of me looking elsewhere, the proprietor suggested that I move there. The rent was affordable, and it was on the opposite side of town so no one should be looking for me there.

Reclamation Process

Several generous individuals and organizations known to the proprietor donated furniture and other items for the apartment. Not long after I'd moved into Victory House, the proprietor had purchased a television for me, and I'd bought a laptop and a cell phone, so I had all the essentials to start my life again.

The brick building dated back to the 1950s. My entry was at the rear, and my apartment was on the second floor. The proprietor, now my landlord, walked with me up the stairs, handed me the keys, and allowed me to open the door.

It opened across from the bathroom. The bedroom was to the left, and back to the right was the kitchen. And this is where it gets interesting. It had a dining room, a living room, and a front room. But instead of being constructed in a pattern, each room adjoined the other in a row. The entrance to the front of my apartment was through a door in the dining room, which opened to steps leading down to the front door of the building.

After placing the boxes and bags in their designated areas, I sat with a plate from the caterer, ate, watched television, and fell asleep in the safety of my new apartment. How the boss had found me was still perplexing. Nobody had known of my whereabouts since the fire. Nonetheless, I was safe and secure for the time being.

~

Now that my life was back on track, it was crucial to use the time before me to settle in and handle unfinished business. Most of my shopping would be done online, from groceries to the shirts on my back, unless I used Uber to go to Walmart to get specific items. In a short time, food filled my refrigerator (the caterer would still deliver if asked), clothes filled my closet, and my office was ready for business. With each day, the atmosphere was proving to be beneficial to my serenity and continued recovery efforts.

The Victory House—the timely blessing that it was— had saved me from ending up on the streets, which I believe has always been another favor from God. Having my own space, not just a bedroom, and returning to the world on my own empowered me even more.

Now, the first order of business was to check in on the house to assess the damage done by the fire.

During this process, I received a letter from the city informing me of deficiencies found on my house and property. All defects, if not addressed by a certain date, amounted to my home being condemned. Upon contacting the city, I spoke with a pleasant person who explained what had happened and how the notice had come to be. My nosy neighbor, who had come out of his house to investigate the real estate agent and me when we first looked at the house, had called in a complaint. We never did get along, but the constant activity—people coming and going all through the night—didn't help. I'm sure that's why they called. And after that call, the city had come to inspect. That's when they identified the defects.

The individual I spoke with also informed me, after I asked, that a notice had been placed on the front door, displaying the property's status. I asked if it had my present address on it, to which she answered yes. That's how Link found me. Willie was still living there. They'd gone back after the fire because they had nowhere else to go at the time. They saw the notice and knew Link was looking for me. Willie gave Link my address, and that solved the mystery.

Though the property was near to being condemned, Willie refused to leave the premises, even after all the utilities had been discontinued. How someone can live in a house for months without utilities is beyond me. Nevertheless, Willie was still there and had to go. After speaking with the proprietor, who explained my options, I began the eviction process immediately.

On the day they were to be gone, I really didn't think they would be when the city inspector and I met at the house. When the side door opened, I could feel an atmosphere void of tension and apprehension. I walked in, looked around, and could immediately tell that the house-guest had left.

The desired conclusion to phase five.

SEVERAL MONTHS AFTER THE FACT, I was now in a position to handle the processing of the claim with the homeowners' insurance company, which asked only a few questions and then began the process immediately. It was left to me to find a construction company, which I did promptly in preparation for the start of the restoration. Having a clear head—not being spaced out or cognitively impaired—allowed me to handle everything with the highest efficiency possible. It would be a couple of months before anything started, so that gave me time to focus on other aspects of my life while waiting.

My finances and credit had suffered tremendously during those years of my extracurricular activities and the automobile accidents. Later, the bills for the EMS rides and emergency room visits would arrive. Addressing the most urgent first, I established a plan to pay each agency as soon as possible. The way in which I began repairing my credit was uncommon and more troublesome than helpful in the beginning, but it eventually worked out to my advantage. Every aspect of reentering society and repairing the devastation from my past was fitting into place perfectly. It wasn't happening as quickly as I wanted, but it was efficient, nonetheless.

When the approval notification for the insurance claim came, I notified the contractor immediately. We agreed upon a payment schedule, with me as the intermediary between the two, and work on the house began three weeks later. If the insurance claim funds run out, the balance of the costs would be my responsibility. Normally, that would have given me pause, but in this case, I had made up my mind to sell the house and use any proceeds to pay off the balance. I wasn't aware of how many layers of stress I had borne for so many years. With every positive thing happening, another layer of stress faded, making any burdens that remained lighter.

Still Quiet Deeds

My vigilance to stay the course did not waver as the wheels of reconstruction turned slowly day by day. It did require patience, which I now had in abundance. Being still quieted my mind, allowing me not only to focus on handling my entrusted business but also to allow God time to work out intricacies behind the scenes on my behalf, Psalm 46:10.

I knew it would take time to sort everything out; I had made quite a mess and put off many things. So, of those that remained, what were the issues that required my immediate attention?

First and foremost, I would resume using Ancestry.com to locate and connect with my biological family.

Before delving into my campaign to find my blood relatives, I received a phone call from my former housemate at the Victory House. My friend had received the manager title due to their extended stay and knowledge of operations, which was a positive nod indeed. Anyway, during the call, my former housemate told me that Link had come by Victory House and asked for me.

"What?" I asked. I couldn't believe what was said.

Although it was the time I'd arranged for Link to return for payment, I didn't think they would actually return. Then, the manager continued to tell me about the conversation with the boss.

"I told him, when you came by that weekend, it made Mister Anthony mad, prompting their relocation the following weekend." The manager had skillfully dispelled a potentially volatile situation with wisdom and wit—an astute achievement indeed, for which I owe gratitude.

I never saw or heard about Link again.

MY DEDICATION to finding my relatives, specifically my mother, was tenacious. I learned to navigate Ancestry's website and began building a family tree with the information I had gathered earlier. Unfortunately, my father's name was not on my birth certificate, so I had no name as a reference for DNA matches on my paternal side.

Though excited, I was a bit hesitant about reaching out to a stranger and saying, "Hi, I'm your son. Nice to meet you!" What might they think of me?

But in the end, it didn't matter. I wanted to connect with my family. So when I gathered the courage, I called the person with the closest DNA match to mine.

It had long been my desire to know who my people are, and now the moment had come to be united with them. The woman I called put me at ease instantly with the sound of her voice. When we spoke, it was as if she was hugging me with her words. After I attempted to provide any information I had gathered and ultimately shared my search focus, she regrettably informed me that my mother was deceased.

In retrospect, I wish I had begun my search sooner. Maybe I would have found her and gotten to know her before she passed.

She did inform me that, of my mother's many brothers, all were gone save one—her father.

I have an uncle who is still alive? I thought, a surge of excitement rising within me. My heartbeat quickened as she continued speaking. I maintained my composure throughout our conversation, aiming not to appear overly eager. However, when she disclosed his location, my excitement surged once again. By the end of our conversation, a weight I'd long carried seemed to dissipate like morning mist. Plans began immediately to visit my uncle at the onset of the new year— though I like to think it was not solely my doing. Indeed, it seemed providential: a new year, a new beginning, and a newfound family. God planned it that way.

~

MY NEWLY FOUND cousin also informed me that I had a sister and that she happened to live in a city close to mine. My heart started beating fast again. *I have a sister?* I thought. That was a complete and utter shock. Good though it was, I hadn't expected to find someone that close to me besides my mother.

"What's her name?" I asked excitedly. When she told me, I paused to consider what might have prompted our mother to give us the names she did. Ultimately, I concluded that she had an intuitive side that she drew her inspiration from.

After receiving my sister's information, I immediately reached out, knowing she would be able to tell me more about our mother and herself. My cousin informed her of my existence and sudden appearance, so she was expecting my call. She had been unaware of my existence as well. We were both overcome with excitement as the conversation ranged from "What do you look like?" to "Can I come and visit you?"

Of course!

We arranged a meeting, and my nerves were a wreck until the day arrived.

When my phone rang, it was her, signaling that she had arrived at my location. I ran down the steps to the back door, swung it open, and then took a moment to gather myself before walking to the car to meet her. Her smile could brighten the darkest of nights, and she had the most delightful personality. I didn't expect her to look so frail, nor did I know she had physical limitations—a complication experienced at birth. Nevertheless, our meeting was so joyous that nothing else mattered. We had finally connected as siblings.

She began to visit me periodically, sometimes to talk and sometimes maybe to share a meal. With each visit, as she spoke, I learned much about the mother I had longed to find. Unfortunately, some information shared about her was not favorable. As it turned out, Mother had a substance use disorder as well. Her choice was alcohol, and my sister, in confidence, shared many struggles that she had endured living with her. When the discussion turned to me, I could only thank God that our mother put me up for adoption. Maybe God granted her a moment of clarity, and she decided not to abort me or make me suffer with her.

Our visits continued, though we always met at my apartment and never hers. I asked her about that once, but she outtalked me and changed the subject. As she continued sharing about her life, she slowly and subtly began inquiring about mine. Holding to my commitment to honesty, I told her everything about me, primarily to see how it would be received. The reception can depend on the person I tell my business to. Her response, though at first surprise, quickly flowed into acceptance. My sister also possessed an endearing spirit, I suppose brought about by her struggle to overcome her disability and live a productive life.

That spirit slowly began to emerge when she started telling me to do things that I had already initiated or already knew to do. She began treating and speaking to me like my big sister. My frustration reemerged with her continued attempts until our conversations became less cheerful. Her slight retreat was noticeable, but her continued willingness to introduce me to specific get-rich-quick opportunities became annoying. While I was working on my final wishes one day, my phone rang, and it was her. Of course, I answered, and we began talking. She asked me what I was doing, and I told her.

"You should hold off on that for a while," she said.

What would make someone I barely know tell me to hold off on making my final arrangements? To me, there was only one answer to that question. She was signifying that I needed help or directions, so my anger made me put her in her place and end the call instantly. How dare she!

Several days went by, then weeks. Into the second month, she had still never called or visited me again. When her birthday came, I tried to call, but she had blocked my number. On another occasion, I was attempting to extend an olive branch, but she still had my number blocked.

We didn't see or speak to each other again for a long time. At least I know I tried.

One day, after a year had passed, I decided to contact my cousin to inquire about her well-being and to update her of my attempts to contact my sister. This time, her words embraced me a little tighter and were forthright in their message. When my cousin gave me my sister's new number, I must confess, my nerves tingled with excitement. Nevertheless, I exercised restraint, waiting until her forthcoming birthday to call—I planned to surprise her that way.

She isn't answering. Why isn't she answering? I thought. Taking care not to seem too anxious, I couldn't decide whether to leave a message or not. She didn't know my new number, so she would only know it was me if my name showed on her caller ID. I decided to leave a message; it was the right thing to do. Plus, if I hadn't and she called me back, she would ask me why I didn't leave a message.

I went on to find something to occupy my time, hoping she would call back soon. One day, as I began to walk past my cell phone, something told me to pick it up to check for missed calls or messages. When I did, I was overjoyed to see that my sister had texted me back. We then went on to speak with each other on the phone. She returned my call, and our conversation was filled with joy again.

So that was how I met my biological sister and what happened between us. Someone told me that sometimes, when those who are adopted find their biological family, they might encounter rejection or a family member who is not enthusiastic about someone new joining their family. Nevertheless, even after our falling-out, we did as siblings should do: we understood, forgave, accepted, and moved on.

IMAGINE yourself pulling your suitcases out of storage, then standing in front of your closet undecided on what clothes to pack. *Should I wear this, or what about that? Will it be cold where my uncle lives, and if so, which coat should I take?* I finally figured everything out in the end and arranged my departure with an Uber that took me to the bus terminal. The bus took me to the big city, and a car picked me up, then took me to the train station, where I waited an hour past my departure time.

Even though the Amtrak was late, I was still eager to have the experience. Finally, the train signaled its arrival with the screech of its brakes. I grabbed my luggage and began walking toward the closest door, thinking I might have packed too much. I struggled up the stairs and through those narrow aisles to the luggage compartments, shoved my bags in, and then walked to my seat. I stayed occupied with my laptop between taking pictures and videos of every-thing. It would have been remiss of me to pass on an oppor-tunity to document one of the most, if not the most, significant moments of my mortal life.

Duplicate Encounter

Though not as fast as the clacks on the high-speed trains in Germany, the clacking of the Amtrak train's wheels over the measured track joints was mesmerizing, nevertheless. We traveled through several states, and I took pictures and videos of train stops, buildings in the distance, and little towns we whizzed by. It was a fascinating experience to embark on such a significant moment of self-discovery, with the train trip being the silver lining because I didn't have to drive.

As the train approached my station, my nerves became excited, but I managed to maintain my composure.

After maneuvering all of that luggage back through those narrow aisles and down the steps to the platform, I hurried into the station. Something had been overlooked in the days leading up to my departure: I didn't know what my uncle looked like, so I needed to figure out who to look for. Looking at the scattered groups of people gathered in certain areas, some walking around going to their destinations, I spotted two people across the room who seemed to be looking for someone. They were looking as hard as I was, so I knew it must have been them. Since I knew my uncle's name, I immediately shouted, "Uncle Calvin, is that you?"

The pandemic was in its first year when I decided to make the trip. As such, the entire population wore protective masks when in public and at certain social events. Both of the individuals turned around at the same time, and when the short one briefly removed his mask, he looked just like me. When he shouted my name, I knew it was my uncle.

He was short like me. In fact, he was a spitting image of me. Or was it the other way around? Either way, I was overjoyed to see and meet him finally, and he was, in turn, overjoyed to see and meet me as well. He introduced me to his grandson, West, my second cousin, and we chatted and laughed as we walked to the car to leave.

"You know, my sister—your mom—never told me she had a son. I didn't find out until my daughter called me and told me about you," was how my uncle started the conversation. From there, he spoke of everything that crossed his mind, often referring to events of the past. He was twenty years my senior, and I could only pray that, if I'm still alive at that age, my memory will be as sharp as that. Unfortunately, I believe that ship sailed several years ago.

Speaking of ships, aside from the extraordinary buildings and bridges shown to me during our impromptu tours, most compelling were the boats and yachts at the docks lining the shore.

Water borders one-third of the state, with inlets and tributaries along the eastern coast. Being around all that water made me reminisce about my days in Okinawa, Japan, when I walked along the beach looking out over the East China Sea. My uncle told me that he had a boat, but it was down for repairs. It was apparent I wouldn't get to ride on it this time because it was the middle of winter, and he was still determining when it would be water-worthy. We would have to schedule that for another date. We decided to wait until the following summer after his road trip, when I hoped to tag along.

I DECIDED to spend the whole week with my uncle. We woke in the mornings; he made breakfast every day, and then we sat down and talked. I was astonished to learn that my uncle still held part-time employment during the workweek. Of course, my trusty laptop kept me occupied during his absence most days, and on the days he didn't have to work, though it was cold, he took me to sightsee and introduced me to other family members who lived close by. Upon leaving each cousin's home, a feeling of complete acceptance rang through me.

These are some of the nicest people I have ever met, I thought to myself.

When Uncle took me down to the basement to look at the pictures he had taken, the number he had in his possession was overwhelming. There were hundreds upon hundreds of photos in dozens of albums and various boxes and bins lying around in all the rooms. My eyes were wide with excitement as he proceeded to describe the scenes in random pictures that jogged his good memory's response.

So pleasant were the days that, when lying down to sleep, though in unfamiliar surroundings, I had no problem falling asleep and staying asleep until morning. During the evenings, as my visit drew to a close, we often sat in the living room as he reminisced about immediate family; only the daughters and grandchildren remained. Though sad at the moment, he spoke of the love and devotion he and his wife had shared.

"She was a beautiful person," my uncle said as he held her picture.

If only I could have met her, but at least over time, I will have access to my uncle's cherished memories of her.

Our parting was, for me, bittersweet. Meeting my uncle, whom I hadn't known existed, and finding out we look alike was an otherworldly experience. The bitter part was leaving my uncle after we had just met. It was also disheartening to leave all the beautiful sights and scenes, boats and yachts, and all of that quiet water. It was like I had ridden a train into a postcard for a vacation destination where my uncle awaited me, and I didn't want to leave.

But, as a good nephew should, I swallowed my disappointment, got in the car, and headed back to the train station. We said our goodbyes, then they left me at the station, and I waited for two hours for my train to arrive. When it finally screeched to a stop, I struggled up the stairs, through the narrow aisles, put my luggage away, and found my seat.

Many thoughts ran through my mind, primarily about my uncle's continuing to live alone in the house much longer. It was becoming a burden to him, but the memories were too precious to let go. Of my uncle's two grandsons, I only met the one who picked me up at the train station with Uncle Calvin. I never saw or spoke to the other cousin, as he didn't consider my visit significant enough to make time to meet me. Any concerns I had about my uncle's well-being were put to rest, knowing his responsible grandson would look after him. There was, however, one more concern. Or maybe it was more like the formulation of a plan.

What if, after selling my house, I moved to where my uncle lives to be around him and get to know him better, to help him and be there in case of emergencies? I thought. That would take some pressure off my young cousin, who had his own life to live. I decided that all of those ideas, wishes, and wants would materialize only in the future, which holds the answers to all.

Finally arriving at my apartment in the early evening, I placed my luggage somewhere out of the way to unpack later. After my whirlwind visit and two train rides, going directly to bed was the only thing left on my mind.

Conclusive Settlement

Compiling all those photos, videos, and audio recordings of my trip seemed an overwhelming task at first. All three of the cell phones I had taken ran out of storage due to the number of pictures and videos. My laptop had more media of my trip as well; I only had to find the pictures' and videos' sequence and organize them chronologically. Looking back through the pictures, watching the videos, and listening to my uncle speak produced a warm feeling within me. With these moments, he will always be with me in spirit, portrait, and voice.

That project, along with other random tasks, occupied my time until spring arrived. Renovations to my house began during the first week of consecutive warm days and continued until completion. Earlier, when the process started, during my stay at Victory House, I had informed the proprietor of my plans to sell my house. The proprietor showed interest and was considering purchasing my home to add to the list of properties they already owned. I was immediately opposed to that possibility; the house was a magnet for conflict. Additionally, I prefer not to do business with friends and associates in order to avoid blame for any defects that might arise after the fact.

The proprietor understood and agreed with my reasoning. Also, due to mortgage company complications, they decided to pull out of the attempt. While discussing the possible purchase, the proprietor mentioned the name of a local real estate agent who would handle everything for them. I was blown away when I heard the name. I told them I had met her before and had found her to be a delightful individual. We had met about two years prior, during my time in the midst of that hell. I had told her that I would get back to her when the time came for me to sell, and that time had finally arrived.

After contacting the agent, who was, by the way, pleasantly surprised to hear from me, we set a date and time to meet. While walking through and looking at the completed renovation, a part of me no longer wanted to sell the house. It almost looked brand new; they had even replaced the garage door and the siding. The next thought that immediately followed was the memory of what had happened there not long before. I quickly shook both thoughts out of my head. As we walked, she explained everything to me in detail, including what to expect and what not to expect, and the sale process began immediately.

PRACTICING patience had become second nature to me; things worked out in their own time. I dared not call the agent to inquire about the status of the listing, but I wanted to. She did, however, eventually send emails with prospective purchasers' responses to their tours of the property. Most were positive, but none came to the point of being captivated enough to commit. It was the main bedroom and sunroom configuration. I was sure of it. Nevertheless, the agent and I agreed that eventually, someone with a similar taste in design would find it to their liking.

After several more people took the tour, finally, someone made an offer, and I was giddy with excitement. Unfortunately, their financing was not approved, and the deal fell through. But I was not going to become disheartened about it. The process had just begun, and it sometimes takes years.

God, please don't let that happen to me, I thought.

Approximately three weeks later, someone else made an

offer. Everything progressed without disruption, and the prospective buyers signaled interest in a closing date. When the scheduling for a closing date drew near, something drastic happened in the neighborhood.

It was on the news, and I'm sure most of the city's residents saw it or heard about the shooting that happened right next to my house. On the day it happened, I was unaware; I was glued to my computer screen as usual. The next day, the real estate agent called to inform me of the incident. She also told me that the buyers had learned of the shooting, changed their minds, and pulled out. My hopes were dashed again, but I still held on to optimism that, in time, someone who didn't know about the shooting would be captured by the appeal of the house and make every effort to buy it.

DURING THIS SUSPENSEFUL WAITING PERIOD, I began making plans to relocate. Since the experience with my dream home had turned out to be a total and complete disaster, I decided that a more reserved dwelling would suit my new life perfectly. My search for a condominium started with me first looking at listings where my uncle lived. Just thinking about relocating to such a beautiful place to live and be with my uncle drove me to search with conviction. Time remained before my house would sell, so I began compiling a list of properties on two real estate websites for future reference.

That plan was consequently changed when one of my uncle's daughters asked him to come live with her family. He expressed his unwillingness to move, saying his decision centered on the timing and personal business. Yet the tenor in his voice gave hints of his thoughts about the whole thing. If my father were living alone in a faraway state with only the young grandsons to look after him between living their lives, I would also be concerned for his well-being. Needless to say, because of her concern, I didn't believe she would stop, and that altered my eventual plans.

Now, as all of that happened, actions taken, phone calls made, paperwork created, emails sent and read, and property tours conducted were all performed by people in some fashion. What happened next I consider another act of God. Exactly three weeks after the second deal fell through, a third prospect showed a distinct interest in the property. Considering my favorite number is three, I became acutely aware of the sequence taking shape. Three interests three weeks apart.

And the third prospect turned out to be the charm.

When the real estate agent called, her greeting was excited, and that excited me.

"I've got some good news," she began.

Being informed that the third prospective buyer had agreed to purchase the house filled my entire body with relief. My arms, legs, hands, and feet relaxed when the agent gave me the news. While quickly falling into a meditative state, my thoughts turned to God, to whom I owed all my gratitude.

Some may question my reasoning and ask, "How do you know it was God?"

First, I refer them to my number three, Romans 8:9 and I Corinthians 6:11, and then I explain to them how God has been with me throughout my life journey.

8

EPILOGUE

Ascertained Stipulation

I was groomed for success, and my path was laid out before me, with countless hours dedicated to developing my passion. What would make someone turn away from the prospect of fame, fortune, and success and choose an uncertain path in life? It was about discovery, with the assurance of a safe return. Spirituality, coupled with the Christian teachings and principles in the Bible, became integral parts of shaping my spiritual being. With this foundation and my unwavering faith and trust, I did not fear the unknown.

That was, until my HIV diagnosis, which effectively derailed my military career and marked the beginning of my life's devastation. Imagine the impact of suddenly being awakened from a deep sleep and being told you have a fatal virus coursing through your veins. It thrust me into an alternate reality, where depression and PTSD settled in during the hours of isolation and involuntary relocation. Disbelief was the most challenging emotion to contend with. Then confusion about the future lay heavy on my mind.

My career was over, and my life was about to end, probably after suffering from debilitating diseases.

Why not try this new drug, crack cocaine, that promises to take all my worries away? I thought.

All I wanted to do was get high and drunk and forget about all of it, and with the new drug, my conscious escape was imminent. To my detriment, I became intricately captured by the unquenchable thirst for this new drug; any attempt to separate proved feeble, and the relentless cravings never ceased. I should have gone home when I had the chance.

As I wallowed in my addiction, both of my parents, years apart, departed from this world, and I wasn't there for them. The burden of that guilt accompanies me like the virus within me, a constant that refuses to fade away. How deep in the darkness must one be that they can't summon the strength to emerge for their dying parents? Yet I can only pray that they have forgiven me. Even after acknowledging my failure to be there for them, the drug persisted in causing damage to my life for years to come.

IN THE INITIAL phase of my dependency, the sole option for support was participating in Alcoholics Anonymous. Although its approach did focus on life choices and changes, this addiction fell beyond any comprehensive recovery strategies. With the advent of Cocaine Anonymous meetings, some stories were meant to encourage, yet some activated cravings due to the details shared. Recollections of the recent past and glimpses into an unchanged future triggered an uncontrollable reaction in my body.

It is crucial to acknowledge, however, that when my attendance at any meeting wavered in any way, my addiction picked up right where it left off. A consequence of that was that each relapse became worse than the one before. Over time, it became clear that attending numerous meetings and hearing various speakers' narratives alone couldn't eliminate the cravings for the substance in my body and the memories in my mind. The only hope left to break free of the captivity, the relentless grip of the crack addiction, was to appeal to God.

Today, my memory fails to recall specific facts about my past, difficult times and circumstances, and where they took place. Some I remember clearly, but I have refrained from entering them into this writing due to repetitiveness or their sensitivity. Of those I remember, in the face of challenging moments, when danger loomed and basic needs were unmet, becoming sober of all substances would have been the desired option.

Yet it was easier said than done.

CONFRONTING struggles with mental health and substance abuse, I found solace in recognizing my life as a testament to God's unwavering presence. As I teetered at the brink of death three times, I was pulled back into the light, echoing the psalmist's words in Psalm 56:12-13. This humbling journey from darkness to light reinforces God's undeniable attentiveness despite my earthly flaws.

The unwavering faith I developed as a child, a testament to a divine answer to my pleas for proof, has served as the bedrock of my life (Romans 8:37-39). It propelled me to embrace life's journey, with its inevitable trials balanced by God's unwavering faithfulness.

THIS PREMISE HOLDS true to this day when faced with a recent disruption in my living arrangements. Necessity compelled me to seek a new residence. A substantial rent increase at the senior living community I moved to after leaving my previous residence disrupted my initial financial plan. This unexpected development has led me to schedule a meeting with the administrator of a prestigious facility in one of the city's affluent suburbs. This new location may provide the familiar sense of community I desire while being more aligned with my current budget.

Turning onto the main street, I was struck by the area's beauty. Two multistory buildings, components of this establishment, sat nestled within The Commons, a quiet residential neighborhood. A tranquil cul-de-sac lined with mature shade trees led to the property. Adjacent to it lay a sprawling golf course, its green expanse adding to the serenity. Meticulously maintained lawns and neatly trimmed shrubs completed the picturesque scene.

After parking my car conveniently near the entrance, I proceeded toward the covered walkway leading into the main building. As I entered, a friendly face greeted me and directed me to the administrator's office. She and I engaged in a detailed discussion regarding the amenities offered, the associated move-in costs, and the facility's emphasis on privacy and discretion. Walking with the administrator, who ably guided me through the softly lit hallways of the property, I admired the beautiful artwork adorning every wall.

The serene atmosphere evoked a sense of comfort and tranquility reminiscent of a sanctuary, reinforcing my hope for a future filled with serenity, security, and a healthy environment in my later years. All of my desires have been fulfilled, my wishes granted, and my needs met. All of my wounds, illnesses, and dependences have been curtailed, leaving nothing more for me to ask. Yet, on behalf of others, my prayers will continue without ceasing.

Witnessing God's boundless love and mercy ignites deep humility and gratitude within me. This extraordinary opportunity, a testament to divine favor, resonates profoundly in my soul. (Matthew 22:37-38) Driven by unwavering resolve and a profound sense of the Divine Power's presence, I now fulfill my solemn promise. With absolute certainty, I depend on this force, offering perpetual reverence and adoration. The Almighty God reigns supreme over all creation, a source of awe that transcends mortal comprehension! In recognizing this divine sovereignty, we find solace and strength. For in God's omnipotence lies the unwavering certainty upon which we can all depend.

THE END

9 798218 488444